MARRIAGE AND DIVORCE

2nd Edition

by
Margaret C. Jasper

Oceana's Legal Almanac Series
Law for the Layperson

2001
Oceana Publications, Inc.
Dobbs Ferry, New York

Library of Congress Control Number 2001135833

ISBN: 0-379-11360-0

Oceana's Legal Almanac Series: Law for the Layperson
ISSN 1075-7376

©2001 by Oceana Publications, Inc.

Manufactured in the United States of America on acid-free paper.

To My Husband Chris

Your love and support
are my motivation and inspiration

-and-

In memory of my son, Jimmy

Table of Contents

CHAPTER 1:
HISTORICAL OVERVIEW

CHAPTER 2:
PRESENT-DAY MARRIAGE LAW

CHAPTER 3:
COHABITATION

CHAPTER 4:
SEPARATION AND DIVORCE

ABOUT THE AUTHOR

MARGARET C. JASPER is an attorney engaged in the general practice of law in South Salem, New York, concentrating in the areas of personal injury and entertainment law. Ms. Jasper holds a Juris Doctor degree from Pace University School of Law, White Plains, New York, is a member of the New York and Connecticut bars, and is certified to practice before the United States District Courts for the Southern and Eastern Districts of New York, the United States Court of Appeals for the Second Circuit, and the United States Supreme Court.

Ms. Jasper has been appointed to the panel of arbitrators of the American Arbitration Association and the law guardian panel for the Family Court of the State of New York, is a member of the Association of Trial Lawyers of America, and is a New York State licensed real estate broker and member of the Westchester County Board of Realtors, operating as Jasper Real Estate, in South Salem, New York. Margaret Jasper maintains a website at http://members.aol.com/JasperLaw.

Ms. Jasper is the author and general editor of the following legal almanacs: Juvenile Justice and Children's Law; Marriage and Divorce; Estate Planning; The Law of Contracts; The Law of Dispute Resolution; Law for the Small Business Owner; The Law of Personal Injury; Real Estate Law for the Homeowner and Broker; Everyday Legal Forms; Dictionary of Selected Legal Terms; The Law of Medical Malpractice; The Law of Product Liability; The Law of No-Fault Insurance; The Law of Immigration; The Law of Libel and Slander; The Law of Buying and Selling; Elder Law; The Right to Die; AIDS Law; The Law of Obscenity and Pornography; The Law of Child Custody; The Law of Debt Collection; Consumer Rights Law; Bankruptcy Law for the Individual Debtor; Victim's Rights Law; Animal Rights Law; Workers' Compensation Law; Employee Rights in the Workplace; Probate Law; Environmental Law; Labor Law; The Americans with Disabilities Act; The Law of Capital Punishment; Education Law; The Law of Violence Against Women; Landlord-Tenant

Law; Insurance Law; Religion and the Law; Commercial Law; Motor Vehicle Law; Social Security Law; The Law of Drunk Driving; The Law of Speech and the First Amendment; Employment Discrimination Under Title VII; Hospital Liability Law; Home Mortgage Law Primer; Copyright Law; Patent Law; Trademark Law; Special Education Law; The Law of Attachment and Garnishment; Banks and their Customers; and Credit Cards and the Law.

INTRODUCTION

Domestic Relations Law, also commonly known as Family or Matrimonial Law, touches almost every person's life at some point, usually in a very personal way. Issues encompassed in this area of the law are those arising from the most basic and private of life experiences. This almanac focuses on the area of Domestic Relations Law that governs marriage and divorce, and necessarily touches on issues related to child custody and support.

The twentieth century brought an unprecedented increase in the marriage failure rate in America. From this unfortunate scenario flows much of the litigation that encompasses Domestic Relations Law. When a couple decides to part, dissolution of the marriage may or may not be such an easy task to accomplish, depending on the laws of the state in which they live. When children are involved, the complications are multiplied.

Individuals who seek a divorce are often represented by an attorney, although it is possible to represent oneself in an uncontested divorce. An uncontested divorce occurs when there are no disagreements between the parties over financial or divorce-related issues, such as child custody and support, division of marital property or spousal support. In addition, one of the parties must either consent to the divorce or fail to appear—i.e. answer the complaint—in the divorce action.

One must be aware that if they proceed without an attorney, they will not have anyone who can advise them on such important issues as property distribution, child custody and support, spousal pensions, etc., and thus may risk losing certain rights. For example, if one spouse is entitled to a pension with his or her employer and the other spouse does not request his or her share of the pension for the duration of the marriage, he or she may lose the right to claim such entitlement in the future.

Thus, if an uncontested divorce becomes contested, or the issues become complicated, the reader is advised to seek legal counsel. The local or state bar association usually provides the public with an attorney referral service if they do not have an attorney. One should request the names of attorneys who specialize in Domestic Relations Law. In addition, parties who meet certain financial criteria may be able to obtain free advice and/or representation by contacting their local legal aid or legal services organizations.

When retaining an attorney in a divorce matter, the client should be aware of the rights and responsibilities that flow from the attorney-client relationship. A Statement of Client's Rights is set forth at Appendix 1 of this almanac and a Statement of Client's Responsibilities is set forth at Appendix 2.

Since state laws vary, this legal almanac presents a general discussion of the various issues related to marriage and divorce. The appendix provides state-specific charts of the various related statutes, as well as sample agreements and other pertinent information and data. The glossary provides the reader with a working knowledge of the definitions of basic legal terms appearing in the almanac.

CHAPTER 1:
HISTORICAL OVERVIEW

EARLY ROMAN LAW

Marriage has been a fundamental institution throughout history. Many of the attributes of modern marriage have their roots in ancient cultures, such as the Hebrew, Greek, and the Roman civilizations. For example, prohibitions against adultery and incest appear in the Old Testament, the Torah and the Talmud.

In 18 B.C., adultery in Rome was widespread. Among the upper classes, marriage was increasingly infrequent and many couples who did marry failed to produce offspring. To try and remedy the moral problems and increase the numbers of the upper classes in Rome, and the population of native Italians in Italy, the Emperor Augustus enacted laws to encourage marriage and having children. These were known as the Julian Marriage Laws.

Under the Julian Marriage Laws, heavier taxes were assessed on unmarried men and women, and awards were offered for marriage and childbearing. The Marriage Laws also included provisions establishing adultery as a crime punishable by exile and confiscation of property. Fathers were permitted to kill daughters and their partners in adultery. Husbands could kill the partners under certain circumstances and were required to divorce adulterous wives.

Under early Roman law, the consent of the parties to live together produced a valid marriage. No forms or ceremonies were necessary. By virtue of the marriage, the husband was granted broad powers over the person and property of his wife. Divorce was similarly accomplished without legal formalities, requiring only that the parties separate with the intention of ending their marriage. However, the power of the husband over the person and property of his wife continued unless formal procedures were undertaken to dissolve that power. Not surprisingly, access to those procedures were available only to the husband and, thus, divorce in the early Roman era was rare.

By the first century A.D., the husband no longer retained such broad powers over the person and property of his wife but, legal procedures to marry and divorce were still not necessary. In part as a result of Christian opposition to the Julian Marriage Laws, they were eventually nearly all repealed or fell into disuse under Constantine and later emperors, including the emperor Justinian.

CANON LAW

It was not until the appearance of Christianity in Europe that changes in marriage and divorce laws began to occur. The canon law, based upon Biblical precepts, replaced the former Roman law in the European countries. Although a private consensual marriage was still valid, the law directed that parties ought to marry only in religious ceremonies after the publication of public notice of the intended marriage between the parties. This notice was known as *banns*. In 1563, at the Council of Trent, the Catholic Church ordained that marriages were not valid unless contracted in the presence of a priest and two witnesses, and divorce was no longer permitted.

Ecclesiastical Law

In England, the Anglican Church retained jurisdiction over the institution of marriage, which was based on the English ecclesiastical, or religious, law. This body of law was very conservative and sought to regulate marriages considerably. Two types of marriage were recognized under the ecclesiastical law—the ceremonial marriage and the consensual marriage, which was similar to that recognized under early Roman law in that only the intent of the parties to be married was needed.

Lord Hardwicke's Act

Such informal marriages continued to be recognized in England until 1753 when Lord Hardwicke's Act was passed. This Act abolished the consensual marriage and instituted certain requirements, including a religious ceremony. Lord Hardwicke's Act also imposed strict regulations concerning marriage between relatives, minimum age requirements, the mental capacity to marry, and the physical ability to procreate. Bigamy was forbidden, and divorce virtually did not exist in England until 1857. In rare circumstances, however, a proceeding was available similar to what is presently known in America as an annulment, a declaration that a valid marriage between the parties never existed.

COLONIAL LAW

The American colonies did not adopt England's ecclesiastical law, but did generally adopt the English form of the marriage ceremony. A type of informal marriage, known in America as common-law marriage, was also validated until its abolition in the majority of the states. The topic of common-law marriage is discussed more fully later in this almanac.

The Catholic and Anglican prohibitions against divorce did not prevail in the largely Protestant colonies, and divorce was treated as a legal matter, available on limited grounds. In the nineteenth century, many states began to enact laws prescribing formal marriage requirements. Today, for example, statutes in every state provide for the issuance of marriage licenses, and in most states, parties wishing to be married are explicitly required to obtain a license.

CHAPTER 2:
PRESENT-DAY MARRIAGE LAW

IN GENERAL

The evolution of the law concerning marriage and divorce in America proceeded very slowly until the 1960's, when rapid development brought significant changes in Domestic Relations law. Much of this change can be attributed to the social revolution of the 1960's and 1970's, which spawned an acceptance of previously condemned conduct, such as premarital sex, cohabitation, divorce, alternate lifestyles, and single parenthood.

More recently, however, a growing segment of the population is seeking a return to what is commonly termed family values. This movement is likely a result of the breakdown of the family unit in America, evidenced by the soaring divorce rates, the escalation of juvenile crime and child abuse, the introduction into society of serious and even fatal sexually transmitted diseases, and the unprecedented number of illegitimate children, many of whom end up in foster care or group homes, lost in a maze of governmental red tape.

The American states have the power to regulate marriage. All jurisdictions have adopted some type of statutory requirements for marriage. Among other things, these statutes set forth the age at which a person can marry, the permissible degree of familial relationship between the parties, licensing requirements, certification requirements for persons who perform the marriage ceremony, and the form of the marriage ceremony itself.

CEREMONIAL MARRIAGE

In all states, parties must acquire a license to marry in order to enter into a ceremonial marriage. Each state sets forth the minimum age requirements for marriage. Although the most common minimum age is set at 18, many states permit individuals to marry at a younger age provided they obtain parental and/or judicial consent.

A table setting forth the statutory minimum age requirements, by state, is set forth at Appendix 3.

In addition, under most state statutes, ceremonial marriages may only be solemnized by ministers, priests and rabbis, or certain other specified public officers, such as justices of the peace. However, if a marriage is solemnized by a person not authorized to perform the marriage, the marriage is nevertheless valid if either or both parties were not aware that the presiding official was not so authorized. Most statutes require two witnesses to the marriage.

Many jurisdictions require some kind of physical examination prior to issuance of a license. In most states, this physical examination is limited to testing for venereal disease, although some states have broadened the test considerably and screen for other diseases, such as sickle cell anemia, tuberculosis, and genetic diseases. Some states also require participation in various types of marital counseling or awareness programs, such as birth control and family planning counseling, as a prerequisite to receiving a marriage license.

Many states have statutes requiring parties who intend to marry to file a formal application for a marriage license, which is then available for public inspection before a license may be issued. Some states do not require any waiting period before issuing a marriage license. However, a three-day waiting period is the most common, and the one adopted by the Uniform Marriage and Divorce Act.

The benefit of such a waiting period is that it allows the parties to contemplate the serious step they are about to take, discourages hasty marriages, and allows for informed decisions in the face of possible physical impediments. In this era of increasing spousal and child abuse and skyrocketing divorce rates, it is considered prudent to present marriage as a commitment that should not be entered into without careful deliberation.

A table setting forth the statutory waiting period before issuance of the license, by state, is set forth at Appendix 4.

In most states, the marriage license expires within a certain time period after issuance if the marriage ceremony does not take place. The duration of validity ranges from 20 days to 1 year, depending on the jurisdiction. In a minority of states, the marriage license does not expire.

A table setting forth the duration of license validity is set forth at Appendix 5.

COMMON-LAW MARRIAGE

A common-law marriage, also known as an informal marriage, is one not solemnized in the ordinary way, but created by an agreement between the parties to marry, followed by cohabitation. As previously discussed, informal marriage had its roots in early Roman law and continued under the ecclesiastical law of England, until abolished in 1753 with the enactment of Lord Hardwicke's Act. Abolition of the common law marriage doctrine resulted from the many abuses of the practice, such as fraudulent claims of marriage and property rights. Thereafter, marriages performed without the required formalities were deemed invalid for all purposes and were considered felonies punishable by death.

Although the American colonies were still under British rule at the time of the passage of Lord Hardwicke's Act, America never adopted the Act. In the colonies, it was generally held that no particular form or ceremony was required for the creation of a valid marriage. There were many practical reasons for this doctrine at the time. In America's early days, travel was dangerous and difficult. Public policy favored recognizing the union of a man and woman who, due to the unavailability of clergy or other official, were unable to enter into a ceremonial marriage. This policy was further supported by a strong emphasis on preventing illegitimacy of the children.

In the nineteenth century, the American states began to enact laws prescribing formal marriage requirements. However, these statutes were merely directory, and their violation did not affect the validity of a marriage. As set forth above, today, statutes in every state provide for the issuance of licenses, and in most states, parties wishing to be married are explicitly required to obtain a marriage license. Common-law marriage has been abolished in thirty-eight states, either by specific legislation or by changing the language of the solemnization formalities of marriage to be construed as mandatory rather than directory.

Today, common-law marriage is recognized under the laws of twelve jurisdictions: Alabama; Colorado; District of Columbia; Iowa; Kansas; Montana; Oklahoma; Pennsylvania; Rhode Island; South Carolina; Texas; and Utah. Although statutes in these jurisdictions vary as to the proof necessary to establish a valid common-law marriage, they all require one essential element—a *present* agreement to be married—normally followed by cohabitation and a *holding out* to the public as husband and wife. The term *holding out* means that the couple represents themselves to the public as a married couple. A couple can fulfill this requirement in various ways, such as by telling people that they are married, by filing joint tax returns, and by stating that they are married on applications, leases, birth certificates and other documents.

The agreement to be *presently* married requires that the parties announce to each other that they are married from that moment forward. While specific words are not required for a valid common-law marriage, there must be evidence of a bona fide meeting of the minds. Because this agreement is usually made without witnesses present, it is generally difficult to prove the existence of such an agreement. If no agreement is proved, there is no common-law marriage.

However, The requisite intent to be presently married may be inferred from circumstantial evidence, such as the parties' cohabitation and holding themselves out as a married couple. It is important to note that mere cohabitation, without a mutual agreement to be married, does not constitute a valid common-law marriage.

Parties to a valid common-law marriage are entitled to all of the usual matrimonial benefits, including property distribution, alimony or maintenance, and all other amenities accorded a lawful spouse. In order to dissolve a common-law marriage, a judicial decree of divorce must be obtained. This is so even if the divorce is sought in a jurisdiction that has abolished the common-law marriage doctrine.

For example, New York does not recognize common-law marriage but Pennsylvania does recognize common-law marriage. If a couple lived together in New York for ten years, they are not legally married even if they considered themselves married. New York would not consider them married under its laws and they would not be required to get a divorce to dissolve their relationship and remarry.

However, if a couple started living together in Pennsylvania, with the mutual agreement to form a common-law marriage, then both Pennsylvania and New York would recognize their marriage as a valid marriage under its laws. If they subsequently moved to New York, they would be required to get a divorce to dissolve their relationship and remarry just as if they had entered into a ceremonial marriage.

Thus, a common-law marriage which is validly entered into in a common-law marriage jurisdiction will be recognized as a valid, legal marriage in a non-common-law marriage jurisdiction.

EXAMPLE: John and Mary live together in Pennsylvania, a state that recognizes common-law marriage. They hold themselves out to their friends and neighbors as being married, and they have agreed between themselves to be married, although they never applied for a marriage license or had an official ceremony. Under Pennsylvania law, John and Mary are considered to be legally married. John subsequently leaves

Mary and moves to New York, where he meets Susan and falls in love. Since he never formally married Mary, John assumes there is no need to file for a divorce. John marries Susan in New York in a formal ceremony before a justice of the peace. Mary finds out about the marriage and files for a divorce in New York based on adultery.

POSSIBLE OUTCOME: The New York court may grant Mary a divorce, ruling that John and Mary were legally married under Pennsylvania law and, therefore, John's subsequent marriage to Susan would be deemed bigamous.

As in England prior to the enactment of Lord Hardwicke's Act, the common-law marriage doctrine in America has led to many abuses, such as fraudulent claims of marriage. Most courts today suspect fraud when parties who could have celebrated a ceremonial marriage claim to have entered into a common-law marriage, especially when the other party objects or the claim is made after the other party's death.

These issues arise even in jurisdictions that have abolished the common-law marriage doctrine since, as previously discussed, those states will still recognize common-law marriages that were validly entered into in a common-law marriage jurisdiction. Persons living together in a state that recognizes common-law marriage, but who do not wish to be married, should sign a statement making it clear that they do not intend to be married.

A table setting forth the common law marriage statutes, by state, is set forth at Appendix 6.

PRENUPTIAL AGREEMENTS

Prior to marriage, a couple may enter into a prenuptial agreement—a contract between the two people in contemplation and consideration of the marriage. The agreement is not binding unless the marriage takes place. A prenuptial agreement attempts to resolve issues of support, distribution of wealth and distribution of property, that may arise in the event of death or failure of the marriage.

Unfortunately, the mere suggestion of the desire for a prenuptial agreement by one of the parties to the marriage can dampen the thrill and romance of the moment because, in part, it presumes the possibility of a divorce even before the couple have exchanged vows.

However, it might be helpful to draw a parallel between a prenuptial agreement and a will. When a person dies without a will, his or her property is distributed according to the state's laws of intestacy, rather than according to the deceased's intentions. Similarly, when a marriage fails, if there is no preexisting agreement between the spouses, they become subject to the state's laws concerning distribution of property and support.

The increase in divorce and remarriage has resulted in a greater demand for prenuptial agreements, particularly when the parties have children from previous marriages. The purpose of many such agreements is to protect the inheritance rights of those children. The parties may waive their rights to benefits which would otherwise pass by intestate succession or by will, including their right to an elective share of the deceased's estate.

A sample prenuptial agreement is set forth at Appendix 7.

Disclosure Requirement

The validity and enforcement of prenuptial agreements are most frequently challenged upon the death of one of the parties or upon dissolution of the marriage. However, in most jurisdictions, prenuptial agreements are favored by public policy and their validity upheld as long as they are properly drafted and executed, and there has been full disclosure by both parties. When a prenuptial agreement is challenged, the courts will scrutinize the facts and circumstances of its execution to be certain the agreement did not violate basic contract principles such as those concerning non-disclosure, fraud, misrepresentation, coercion and overreaching. The Court will also require that such agreements be fair and equitable under the circumstances.

> EXAMPLE: John and Mary execute a prenuptial agreement providing Mary with a small lump sum payment if they divorce. At the time the agreement is signed, Mary does not know that John has a controlling interest as a silent partner in a successful manufacturing business, and John does not volunteer this information. Seven years later, John and Mary separate in contemplation of divorce. Mary's attorney discovers that John owns stock in the manufacturing business worth approximately $1.2 million. John's attorney attempts to enforce the provisions of the prenuptial agreement, arguing that Mary is not entitled to any portion of the value of John's stock.

> POSSIBLE OUTCOME: The court may rule that Mary is entitled to a portion of the value of the stock because John intentionally did not disclose his ownership in the manufacturing business at the time the prenuptial agreement was executed.

Maintenance and Support Provisions

In most instances, a well-written prenuptial agreement can prevail over the states's domestic relations statutes. The agreement cannot, however, circumvent the obligation of a husband and wife to support each other in time of need, or the requirement that parents provide for the support of their children.

> EXAMPLE: John and Mary execute a prenuptial agreement. At the time the agreement is signed, John is the manager of a successful automobile dealership and Mary is a college student. The agreement provides that, in the event of a divorce, John will retain custody of any children of the marriage, and Mary will pay John $25 per week towards the support of each child. Ten years later, Mary has completed her education and has built a successful accounting firm. There is one child of the marriage, John Jr., aged 8. Mary wants a divorce. She agrees to abide by the custody provision of the prenuptial agreement. John takes custody of John Jr., and Mary pays John $25 per week towards the child's support. Two years later, the automobile industry suffers a tremendous downturn, John's business goes bankrupt, and John becomes unemployed. Mary's accounting firm is very successful. John requests Mary to raise the amount of support she provides for John Jr., but Mary refuses based on the prenuptial agreement.

> POSSIBLE OUTCOME: Despite the agreement, the court may rule that Mary must increase her child support payments on behalf of John, Jr., based on her ability to pay and the change in circumstances.

The Uniform Premarital Agreement Act

In 1983, the Uniform Premarital Agreement Act (UPAA) was approved and recommended for enactment in all states by the National Conference of Commissioners on Uniform State Laws. The purpose of the Act is to provide uniformity of treatment of prenuptial agreements throughout the states, and to provide guidelines to follow in drafting such agreements so as to ensure maximum enforceability of the terms of the agreement.

CHAPTER 3:
COHABITATION

IN GENERAL

Many couples have decided to live together without marrying in order to avoid becoming embroiled in legal complications if the relationship fails. The courts have nevertheless entertained some very interesting lawsuits arising from such situations, including palimony suits and common-law marriage claims. Like married couples, unmarried couples also accumulate property during their relationship, and judicial intervention is often needed to resolve property disputes when the couple breaks up. In addition, many unmarried couples are parents, and when they decide to part, issues of child custody and support also flow from that separation.

Although a variety of agreements covering the various relationships, such as prenuptial and cohabitation agreements, have been devised in an attempt to eliminate the foreseeable problems, such agreements often end up in court. The two starry-eyed people who entered into the agreement at the start of the relationship may no longer be seeing eye-to-eye at the end. Depending on the course the relationship followed, one party to the agreement may feel that the terms agreed upon are unfair or no longer valid given the present situation. There is absolutely no ironclad way to predict the future when you are dealing with what boils down to the law of human relationships. Nevertheless, a number of legal rules have been established to protect the interests of all parties involved. In particular, the legislators and the courts are concerned with the well-being of children caught in the middle of such adult disputes.

COHABITATION

Cohabitation is defined as the mutual assumption of those marital rights, duties, and obligations usually manifested by married people, including, but not necessarily dependent on, sexual relations. A lifestyle once illegal in a number of jurisdictions, and looked scornfully upon as "living in sin," cohabitation, or "living together," has become a socially acceptable lifestyle in recent years. In fact, many couples express fear of the marriage commitment without first living together to assess their compatibility. Others simply prefer cohabitation to the formality of marriage.

In recent years, there has been a trend for unmarried couples to seek rights and privileges which were traditionally reserved for married couples, such as family health insurance coverage through their respective employers. Those efforts have generally been unsuccessful except in those more progressive jurisdictions which have adopted domestic partner legislation. There are a few cities which allow unmarried couples to register as domestic partners thus affording them certain benefits previously available only to married couples.

COHABITATION AGREEMENTS

Although the courts of some states have awarded support and distribution of property rights to separating unmarried couples, generally the courts will not do so unless there is an agreement between the parties. *Palimony* is the term commonly used to describe the provision of support or distribution of property arising out of a nonmarital relationship, by court award, settlement, or agreement.

A cohabitation agreement is a contract similar to a prenuptial agreement in that it attempts to define the rights and responsibilities of the parties in the event the relationship is dissolved. However, any provision making such agreement contingent upon the sexual services of either party may cause the agreement to be declared invalid as violative of public policy.

> EXAMPLE: John and Mary execute a cohabitation agreement and begin living together. The agreement provides that Mary will not unreasonably abstain from sexual relations with John during their cohabitation. In return, John agrees that if they separate, he will pay Mary $1,000 per month for one year thereafter. John and Mary separate, and John refuses to pay Mary any money. Mary tries to enforce the cohabitation agreement.

> POSSIBLE OUTCOME: The court may rule that the agreement is invalid because it was contingent on Mary's providing sexual relations and thus violates public policy.

Cohabitation, or living together agreements, can be custom designed to meet a couple's specific desires and needs. As long as the agreement doesn't include clauses concerning sexual services, most courts will uphold its validity under the principles of contract law. A contract is simply an exchange of promises between the parties. You can agree to share all property or keep all property separate. You can agree to share some items and keep other items separate. You can discuss any matter which relates to your relationship.

A sample cohabitation agreement is set forth at Appendix 8.

SAME-SEX MARRIAGE

Case law has consistently held that people of the same sex may not marry, whether or not there exists a statute expressly forbidding the practice. At present, no state allows legal marriage for same-sex partners. The controversy centers around the definition of marriage, which courts have described as a union between a man and a woman with an emphasis on procreation. Many supporters of same-sex marriage maintain that the prohibition is unconstitutional discrimination. Although there has been a considerable amount of litigation concerning this prohibition, the United States Supreme Court has thus far refused to hear cases on the matter. Basically, the courts have left this matter to be resolved through the legislative process.

Another stumbling block in the adoption of same-sex marriage concerns the criminal laws of many states which still forbid certain sexual activities between consenting adults. Although most states have decriminalized sodomy, laws prohibiting sodomy still exist in Alabama, Arkansas, Florida, Idaho, Kansas, Louisiana, Maryland, Massachusetts, Michigan, Minnesota, Mississippi, Missouri, North Carolina, Oklahoma, South Carolina, Texas, Utah and Virginia. In Arkansas, Maryland, Missouri, Oklahoma and Texas, these laws apply only to same-sex partners. The charges range from misdemeanors to felonies and the penalties range from 60 days in jail and a $500 fine to life imprisonment in Idaho. Although these statutes are rarely enforced, the states cannot officially sanction such criminal activity by issuing a marriage license to same-sex partners.

On the other hand, however, some jurisdictions have passed laws which depict a growing tolerance of same-sex relationships. For example, in 1989, San Francisco enacted an ordinance prohibiting discrimination by the city against unmarried couples, regardless of sex, who register with the city as domestic partners. A domestic partnership under the statute arises when two people live together with the desire to share one another's lives in an intimate and committed relationship. More recently, San Francisco was the first jurisdiction to provide health care coverage for sex-change operations for its municipal employees.

In addition, the New York Court of Appeals held that the term family, as it related to the rent and eviction statutes, could include the homosexual partner of a deceased tenant, thus giving the surviving partner noneviction protection.

According to the American Civil Liberties Union, there is a strong possibility that Hawaii will allow same-sex marriages. Thus, the states have been trying to decide how to treat those same-sex couples who do get married in Hawaii within their own jurisdictions should such couples choose to reside in those states. Some opponents of same-sex marriage have been seeking to block recognition of these out-of-state marriages through legislation.

The ACLU's position is that states which enact laws that prevent recognition of out-of-state same-sex marriages violate the "Full Faith and Credit" clause of the U.S. Constitution, which states: "Full Faith and Credit shall be given in each State to the public Acts, Records and judicial Proceedings of every other State." The idea behind this clause was to make sure that in a nation where people could freely move from state to state, each state would respect each others laws.

The ACLU also believes these laws violate equal protection, since they seek to discriminate against homosexual Americans. The laws also violate the right to interstate travel under Supreme Court precedent, which has held that a state cannot discriminate against people entering its territory by imposing unconstitutional conditions on the right to enter.

Anti-same-sex marriage laws fall into three general groups:

1. Laws that say same-sex marriages are "null and void" or that marriage is a union between a man and a woman;

2. Laws that say recognition of a same-sex marriage from another state is prohibited; and

3. Laws that say recognition of any type of out-of-state marriage is allowed only if the couple could have married in the state itself.

A table of states that prevent recognition of an out-of-state same sex marriage license, by statute, is set forth at Appendix 9.

A table of states that do not have laws preventing recognition of an out-of-state same-sex marriage license is set forth at Appendix 10.

CHAPTER 4:
SEPARATION AND DIVORCE

HISTORICAL OVERVIEW

Divorce was not common in early America, reflecting the ecclesiastical history of the institution of marriage. The church, emphasizing the stability of the family, considered marriage a blessed sacrament and forever indissoluble. However, parties were granted a very limited right to divorce, whereby they were permitted to physically separate from each other, for cause, but could not remarry, and each party still maintained financial responsibility for the family.

The Protestant reformers rejected the sacramental character of marriage and asserted the concept of an absolute divorce, but did not allow divorces to take place freely. Maintenance of the family was still the primary focus. Divorce was permitted on limited fault grounds—adultery or malicious desertion—and only the innocent party could remarry.

During the nineteenth century, the development of fault grounds for granting divorce broadened. This required proof in a court of law by the divorcing party that the divorcee had done one of several enumerated things as sufficient grounds for the divorce, for example, proving that the spouse had committed adultery, or some other unsavory act. Judicially created defenses were developed to counter those fault allegations. Nevertheless, it was still very difficult to obtain a divorce, leading to such undesirable behavior as perjury and collusion by the parties seeking to divorce.

The major pressure for divorce reform occurred during the 1960's and 1970's, when emphasis shifted from finding fault—the traditional fault grounds—to finding out whether the marriage had any chance for success. There emerged new non-fault causes for divorce, such as irreconcilable differences, incompatibility, and separation grounds. No-fault divorce eliminated the potentially embarrassing and undesirable requirement of proving fault by providing for the dissolution of a marriage on a finding that the relationship is no longer viable.

Due to the divorce reform movement, divorces are much more freely obtainable today, and a growing number of jurisdictions have abandoned fault as a consideration in granting divorce decrees.

SEPARATION

Separation occurs when a husband and wife cease cohabitation, either by mutual agreement or by judicial decree. Separation does not end a marriage but, in many states, is grounds for a divorce after a specified time period. Parties may enter into a separation agreement in anticipation of a legal separation or divorce. Among other things, the separation agreement usually sets forth provisions concerning child custody, child support, spousal maintenance, and property division.

A sample separation agreement is set forth at Appendix 11.

In general, the terms of the separation agreement survive and govern the parties through the divorce decree unless the decree specifically states that it does not. However, courts will not uphold any provision in a separation agreement that provides for maintenance which is so unconscionably low that the spouse may become a public charge.

> EXAMPLE: John and Mary execute a separation agreement which provides that John will give Mary $50 per month maintenance. Both John and Mary are working. During their separation, Mary's company issues massive layoffs. Mary loses her job and cannot find alternative employment. Her earnings from unemployment insurance are minimal, and she is unable to support herself. On the other hand, John is doing very well financially. Mary asks John to increase her monthly maintenance until she can get back on her feet. John refuses based on the maintenance provision of the separation agreement.

> POSSIBLE OUTCOME: The court may rule that John must increase his maintenance payments because they are so unconscionably low that Mary is in danger of becoming a public charge.

In addition, child custody and support provisions are never binding on a court, although they may be considered.

> EXAMPLE: John and Mary execute a separation agreement which provides that Mary will retain custody of their two minor children, aged 4 and 6. John subsequently discovers that Mary has developed a drug and alcohol addiction, and has been known to leave the children alone for days at a time while she goes on drinking binges. John goes to Mary's house to confront her and discovers the children home alone. He takes the children and leaves a note for Mary advising her that he is taking over custody and will no longer pay child support. Mary goes to court to enforce the custody and support provisions of the separation agreement.

POSSIBLE OUTCOME: Based on the facts, and the best interest of the children, the court may rule that custody reverts to John and child support is canceled. In addition, the court may require Mary to pay child support to John.

ANNULMENT

Unlike a divorce, which terminates a marriage, an annulment establishes that a marriage never existed. Historically, annulment was viewed as the less controversial alternative to dissolution of a marriage. Although there are statutory grounds for the annulment of a marriage, there have been cases where annulments were granted on non-statutory bases, such as religious opposition to divorce, or where a marriage was of very short duration and did not involve children.

A grant of annulment requires a determination that a marriage is either void or voidable.

Void Marriage

A void marriage is one which is contrary to a state's strong public policy, such as an incestuous marriage or an intentionally bigamous marriage, and usually needs no formal judicial action or declaration to establish its invalidity.

EXAMPLE: John and Mary have been married for five years. John goes on an extended business trip to Las Vegas, where he meets Susan. After a whirlwind romance, John and Susan marry. John does not tell Susan that he is already legally married to Mary.

OUTCOME: John's marriage to Susan is bigamous and, therefore, void. Susan can remarry without having to file for a divorce from John since legally they are considered as never having been married.

A void marriage cannot be ratified, or validated, even following the removal of the defect that caused the marriage to be void. However, it should be noted that cohabitation following removal of the defect can still lead to the establishment of a valid common-law marriage in some jurisdictions.

Parties to a void marriage can separate, without consequence, and do not have to seek a judicial decree ending the marriage. Nevertheless, some courts entertain actions to terminate void marriages for the sole purpose of providing certainty to the invalidity of the marriage, in order to resolve issues such as those relating to property or children, by granting a judicial declaration of invalidity or nullity. In addition, third parties can attack a void marriage, even after the death of one or both of the parties, such as in a will contest.

Voidable Marriage

A voidable marriage is one which is valid when entered into, and which remains valid until one of the parties to the marriage seeks a judicial determination that the marriage is void. An annulment can no longer take place after the voidable marriage has been ratified, since a ratified voidable marriage is considered valid from its inception.

A voidable marriage usually impinges on some lesser public policy that existed before the marriage was formed, as opposed to divorce, where the defect occurs after the formation of the marriage. There are approximately six grounds upon which an annulment can be granted, including failure of a party to meet the statutory age requirement; lack of mental capacity, innocent bigamy; fraud; force; and physical incapacity for sex.

A voidable marriage can be ratified, or validated, by the conduct of the parties following the removal of the defect that caused the marriage to be voidable. For example, if the potential ground for annulment is age, once the under-aged party reaches the statutory age for marriage and the parties continue their relationship, that marriage is a valid, legal marriage for all purposes. An annulment can no longer take place after the voidable marriage has been ratified or after the death of a party to the marriage. Although a ratified voidable marriage is considered valid from its inception, a voidable marriage that has been annulled by judicial decree is deemed to have been invalid from its inception.

> EXAMPLE: John, who is 18 and Mary, who is 16, want to get married. The law provides, however, that one must be at least 18 years of age to marry without parental consent. Although Mary's parents refuse to consent to the marriage, the couple does marry, providing false documentation as to Mary's age.

> OUTCOME: If Mary changes her mind about the marriage before turning 18, she can petition the court for an annulment based on lack of age and, once annulled by judicial decree, the marriage will have been deemed invalid from its inception. However, if Mary and John remain married after Mary becomes of legal age, their marriage is considered ratified and valid from its inception.

DIVORCE

Fault Grounds

Although there is a growing trend to eliminate fault as a consideration in granting a divorce, most states have retained traditional fault grounds for divorce, while incorporating some form of no-fault provision in their divorce law. For example, some states that are not considered no-fault jurisdictions, such as New York, will grant a divorce based upon separation for a specified period of time. In practical terms, this is also a no-fault ground.

The primary fault grounds for divorce recognized in most jurisdictions are adultery, cruelty, abandonment, and constructive abandonment. Grounds for both divorce and separation must be proven by a fair preponderance of the evidence. Since each jurisdiction varies with respect to the admissibility of evidence in matrimonial matters, the laws of the state in which the action is pending should be consulted as to the requirements needed to prove a particular ground.

A table setting forth the legal grounds for divorce, by state, is set forth at Appendix 12.

Adultery

Adultery is the voluntary sexual intercourse of a married person with a person other than the offender's husband or wife. Adultery usually requires as proof the testimony of a third party. It is not necessary to provide eyewitness testimony to the actual act of adultery. Rather, adultery is usually proven by circumstantial evidence, such as entering and exiting a hotel with a person of the opposite sex. Sometimes a private detective is called upon to provide testimony after conducting surveillance of the adulterous spouse.

Acts of adultery may also qualify as acts of cruelty and entitle the spouse seeking the divorce to maintain a divorce action based on cruelty rather than adultery. This may be a way of obtaining the divorce without the necessity of additional evidence—e.g., third party testimony—as is required to prove adultery.

Cruelty

Cruelty is the intentional and malicious infliction of physical or mental suffering on one's spouse. Cruelty is usually more difficult to prove than adultery, although jurisdictions vary in the degree of proof needed.

Usually, one instance of cruelty would not be enough to support a divorce action. For a divorce based on the ground of cruelty, it is generally required that there be a pattern of cruelty over an extended period of time, particularly when the marriage is of long duration.

EXAMPLE: John and Mary have been married for 20 years. One night, John goes out for a drink with a co-worker after a particularly hard day at the office. He arrives home late for dinner and Mary smells liquor on his breath. Mary accuses John of infidelity and they argue. John becomes increasingly incensed over the false accusations and reaches out and slaps Mary across her face. This is the first and only time John ever strikes Mary. Mary, who has been unhappy in the marriage for some time, leaves John and files for divorce based on cruelty, citing that one incident. John opposes the divorce.

POSSIBLE OUTCOME: The court may rule that the facts do not support a finding of cruelty, particularly since John and Mary's marriage is a lengthy one.

Nevertheless, one particularly malicious act of cruelty may suffice in some jurisdictions. The main focus is the effect upon the victim and a showing that the acts complained of have had an adverse effect upon the physical or mental welfare of the victim. Mental cruelty is more difficult to prove than physical cruelty, and some jurisdictions require the corroboration of a psychiatrist.

Abandonment

Abandonment is the willful and intentional desertion of a spouse, without the consent of the spouse, and without any intention of returning to the spouse. Most states require that the abandonment continue, without cohabitation or sexual relations, for a specified period of time. In addition, to be granted a divorce based on the ground of abandonment, the spouse seeking the divorce cannot have provoked the abandonment.

EXAMPLE: John and Mary have been married for 5 years. John is abusive, but Mary is attempting to make the marriage work. One evening, John comes home drunk and beats Mary severely, requiring her hospitalization. Mary, afraid to return home after her discharge from the hospital, stays with relatives but tells John she will return to him if he seeks counseling. John files for a divorce based on abandonment. Mary, who still loves John and wants to make the marriage work, opposes the divorce.

POSSIBLE OUTCOME: The court may rule that John is not entitled to a divorce based on abandonment because his physical violence provoked Mary into leaving.

Constructive Abandonment

Constructive abandonment occurs when one spouse is ready and willing to engage in sexual relations but the other spouse refuses, without cause, to do so. The spouse who is responsible for the cessation of sexual relations cannot maintain a cause of action for divorce on this ground.

Imprisonment

An action for divorce may be maintained where the Defendant is imprisoned for a period of time, e.g., at least three consecutive years. The imprisonment must have commenced after the date of the marriage and the Defendant must still be in prison when the divorce action is commenced.

Defenses

Some states still retain certain defenses available to defeat a divorce action, including condonation, recrimination, procurement, provocation, and justification.

For example, in defense of an adultery claim, condonation occurs when the offending spouse is forgiven and the parties continue to live together after discovery of the adultery, while recrimination occurs when the other spouse commits adultery also. Procurement may occur if one spouse causes the offense underlying the divorce action, such as by entrapment.

A defense to abandonment may be that cruel and inhuman treatment forced the spouse to leave, thus justifying the abandonment. It is also a defense to constructive abandonment if the spouse is medically unable to have sexual relations.

It is important to note, however, that most states have limited or eliminated the traditional defenses to make it easier to obtain a divorce decree. The rationale behind limiting divorce defenses is that a denial of divorce clearly does not save a marriage, but prolongs the painful process.

No-Fault Divorce Grounds

There are approximately five classifications of no-fault divorce grounds, including: (1) incompatibility; (2) proof of a dead marriage, commonly referred to as irretrievable breakdown or irreconcilable differences; (3) separation by agreement for a certain period of time; (4) separation under irretrievable breakdown conditions for a specified period of time, with or without agreement or voluntariness; and (5) long-term absence of a spouse, leading to the presumption of his or her death. Some states that have adopted no-fault legislation require attempts at reconciliation prior to bringing an action.

Some jurisdictions, such as New York, which have maintained the traditional fault requirements for divorce, also allow for a "conversion divorce"—the closest thing to a no-fault divorce. A conversion divorce is based on a separation agreement. The separation agreement must be signed by the parties, notarized, and filed with the County Clerk in the county where one of the parties resides. The parties must live separate and apart for a certain period of time—e.g. at least 1 year in New York—according to the terms and conditions of the separation agreement, after which time they may maintain an action for divorce based on the separation agreement.

Maintaining a Divorce Action

Residency Requirements

Almost every jurisdiction has a residency requirement, generally ranging from 30 days to one year. If a divorce is granted based on a false residency claim, the divorce decree can be attacked for lack of jurisdiction by the spouse seeking to resist the divorce. Lack of jurisdiction means that the court did not have the legal authority to entertain the divorce action.

If residency is attacked, the court will consider certain factors to determine whether the party seeking the divorce was a bona fide resident of the state. Relevant factors include: acquisition of a driver's license in the jurisdiction; registration to vote in the jurisdiction; purchase of real property in the jurisdiction; or other proof of residency in the jurisdiction, such as a lease.

A table containing the residency requirements for each of the states is set forth at Appendix 13.

Filing the Papers

The first step in filing a divorce action is preparing the Summons and Complaint for Divorce. In general, an attorney is retained to prepare the necessary papers, however, if the divorce is uncontested, an individual may be able to maintain the divorce action without representation. Nevertheless, if the divorce becomes contested or there are any complications which arise, it would be prudent to consult an attorney.

The Summons and Complaint sets forth the grounds for the divorce and the relief requested, and gives notice to the defendant that the plaintiff is seeking a divorce. The plaintiff may be required to "verify" the Complaint—i.e., swear under oath that the allegations contained in the Complaint are true. The Summons and Complaint is usually filed with the County Clerk in the county where one of the parties to the action resides.

A sample Summons and Verified Complaint for Divorce is set forth at Appendix 14.

There are certain court filing fees which must be paid along with the filing of the Summons and Complaint at the Clerk's office. However, individuals who do not have the necessary financial resources to pay the filing fees are not precluded from maintaining a divorce action. In general, an indigent person may apply to the Court for poor person status, in which case the Court will enter a "Poor Person Order" dispensing with court costs and filing fees.

A sample Poor Person Order is set forth at Appendix 15.

After the filing of the Summons and Complaint, the papers are generally served upon the Defendant. In some jurisdictions, the sheriff's office will serve papers. There are also professional process servers who may be hired to serve the papers. Usually, the person serving the papers must be over the age of 18 and not a party to the action.

If the Defendant does not contest the divorce, he or she generally does not appear in the action or otherwise answer the Summons and Complaint, and a default judgment of divorce will be entered once all of the appropriate forms are submitted. The plaintiff generally must serve a copy of the final judgment of divorce on the defendant.

If the plaintiff is seeking maintenance, custody, visitation, or distribution of property, the court may require a hearing unless there is a written agreement or prior court order. In addition, if the plaintiff is seeking exclusive occupancy of the marital home, he or she must assert that their spouse is not living in the marital home; otherwise a hearing may also be ordered.

If the Defendant contests the divorce or some of the relief being sought, e.g., child custody and support, maintenance, etc., he or she must serve an Answer to the Complaint within a prescribed period of time. In this case, the parties are advised to retain attorneys because a divorce and custody trial can become very complicated.

After a judgment of divorce is entered, the state may require a Certificate of Dissolution of Marriage to be filed with the County Clerk's office which provides the details of the marriage and its dissolution.

A sample Certificate of Dissolution of Marriage is set forth at Appendix 16.

CHAPTER 5:
PROPERTY DISTRIBUTION AND FINANCIAL ISSUES

OVERVIEW

The divorce reform movement has had a significant impact on the economic issues surrounding divorce, which include property distribution, maintenance, and support. Prior to reform, many states were title states, meaning that property was distributed according to who held title in the property. The majority of the jurisdictions have now adopted equitable distribution legislation to settle the marital estate following divorce, while nine states have adopted community property legislation.

A table specifying each jurisdiction's property division law is set forth at Appendix 17.

MARITAL PROPERTY

The term "marital property" has not been uniformly defined among the states, but is generally used to refer to any property that is acquired from the date of marriage to the date a matrimonial action is commenced. Marital property may include real and personal property, including cars, bank accounts, jewelry, investments, and household items. Premarital real property which is retitled in joint names after marriage may also be considered marital property.

During the course of the proceeding, the parties are generally required to complete a financial disclosure form setting forth all of their income, assets, liabilities, and expenses.

A sample Financial Disclosure Affidavit is set forth at Appendix 18.

Courts have also ruled in some jurisdictions that business interests—including a professional license, such as a license to practice law or medicine—are also subject to distribution as marital property.

EXAMPLE: John and Mary fall in love and marry while they are college students. Subsequently, they both graduate from college with degrees. John accepts a position as a computer programmer at a local company, while Mary pursues further education in the field of medicine. John works and supports Mary while she completes the requirements for her medical degree. After completing many years of schooling and her residency requirements, Mary obtains her medical license and establishes a successful practice as a pediatrician. Meanwhile, however, she has grown apart from John, and she now seeks a divorce.

POSSIBLE OUTCOME: The court may rule that Mary's license to practice medicine is subject to equitable distribution and that John is entitled to a portion of the value of that license.

Employee pensions are also subject to distribution unless the parties agree to waive their rights in the other spouse's pension plan. In general, a spouse is usually entitled to a percentage of the other spouse's pension calculated from the period of the inception of the marriage to the date the action for divorce was filed. However, pension funds are not distributed until the employee spouse retires or the parties' reach a certain age. A Qualified Domestic Relations Order is usually presented to the Court for signature and given to the Pension Plan Administrator so that the funds can be disbursed appropriately in the future.

A sample Qualified Domestic Relations Order (QDRO) is set forth at Appendix 19.

SEPARATE PROPERTY

Separate property generally refers to the property owned by either spouse before marriage, as well as property acquired by either spouse after marriage by gift or inheritance.

EXAMPLE: John and Mary have been married for 10 years. John's grandmother dies and leaves him $10,000, which John places in a separate bank account in his own name. John and Mary subsequently divorce. Other than their home, there is no marital property to divide. Mary seeks a portion of John's bank account in the divorce judgment.

POSSIBLE OUTCOME: The court may rule that the bank account is separate property and Mary is not entitled to any portion of it, since John acquired the money in the account by inheritance and kept it separate during the marriage.

Separate property is retained by the spouse who owns it and is not subject to distribution upon divorce. However, if separate property is mixed with marital property, it will likely lose its separate identity for the purposes of distribution. In the example above, if John deposited his all or part of his $10,000 inheritance in a joint bank account commingled with Mary's money, it is likely that it would be considered marital property and subject to distribution. Consequently, it is important to keep accurate records of all separate property if one wishes to maintain control and ownership over such property upon dissolution of the marriage.

EQUITABLE DISTRIBUTION LAW

In equitable distribution states, the court has the power to distribute marital property equitably upon divorce, whether the property is jointly or individually held. Equitable distribution is not equal distribution. The courts use a number of factors in determining how to equitably distribute marital property. Although the factors considered may differ from state to state, they generally include: the duration of the marriage; the age and health of both parties; the direct and indirect contributions of each party to the marriage; the wasteful dissipation of marital assets by either party; and the financial circumstances of the parties following the divorce.

COMMUNITY PROPERTY LAW

The distribution provisions under the laws of the nine community property states are by no means uniform, but there are general community property principles. All property owned by either spouse at the time of a divorce is generally presumed to be community property, unless it can be proven separate. When the spouses cannot document ownership or the source of funds used to acquire separate property, that property is considered commingled and is thrown into the community property pot for distribution at the time of divorce. Commingling, or mixing separate property with community property, makes it impossible for that property to ever again be classified as separate property. Therefore, it is critical that each party keep accurate records of their separate property, including any replacements of such property.

Community property, including earnings, is considered to be owned in common by the husband and wife, each having an undivided one half interest by reason of their marital status. Most community property states also take into consideration certain factors in distributing community property. However, California, considered a pioneer in divorce reform, usually requires an equal distribution of community property unless the spouses agree otherwise.

MARITAL FAULT

Some states, whether operating under community property or equitable distribution law, permit the court to consider the issue of marital fault or misconduct when distributing marital property upon divorce. When marital fault is proven, depending on the degree of misconduct, the court has the power to divide the marital property in favor of the innocent spouse. States differ in the weight they may assign marital fault, some requiring the conduct to be particularly egregious in order to depart from the usual manner of distributing property.

THE UNIFORM MARITAL PROPERTY ACT

The Uniform Marital Property Act (UMPA or the Act) was approved by the National Conference of Commissioners on Uniform State Laws (NCCUSL) in 1983 and is available as both a model to the states in drafting and reforming their divorce laws, and as a model for parties who wish to enter into a property distribution agreement during marriage. The UMPA is based on the principle that spouses share the property they acquire during marriage, including income, regardless of which spouse contributes the property. All such property is referred to as marital property under the Act.

Under the UMPA, property brought into the marriage or acquired afterward by gift or inheritance remains individual property, including its appreciation value. Any income derived from such property, however, becomes marital property. The Act does not attempt to advise courts on how to distribute the marital property, but relies on each court's determination under its property distribution system.

ALIMONY/MAINTENANCE

Although some jurisdictions have retained the term "alimony," most jurisdictions have substituted the term "maintenance" to describe the support of a spouse during and following dissolution proceedings. Spousal support provisions have undergone major revision as a result of the divorce reform movement. Prior to the adoption of community property and equitable distribution laws, the payment of alimony was often awarded to a wife until her death or remarriage. Historically, it was quite common for the husband to hold most, if not all, property in his individual name, and under the title form of distribution, he retained all such property upon divorce. Alimony was designed to support the wife, who often did not work outside the home, and who had little or no chance to earn a living, much less maintain the standard of living she enjoyed when married.

The adoption of community property and equitable distribution laws gave courts the ability to award substantial marital assets to either spouse, regardless of the title in which the property was held, thereby reducing the need for a long-term alimony or maintenance award. Today, maintenance is typically awarded for a limited time only, if at all, unless the marriage was of long duration and the recipient spouse is likely to be unemployable for reasons such as age.

Maintenance is generally available to either spouse and is awarded based upon a number of factors involving the ability of the payor spouse and the needs of the recipient spouse. Relevant factors may include the standard of living enjoyed by the recipient spouse prior to separation, the share of property distribution awarded to the recipient spouse and the likelihood that such property will produce income, and the age, health, and earning capacity of the recipient spouse.

Although most states do not consider fault or marital misconduct in the decision to award maintenance, some states still provide that marital misconduct is an absolute bar to any such award.

A table setting forth the factors considered in awarding spousal support is set forth at Appendix 20.

CHAPTER 6:
CHILD SUPPORT

OVERVIEW

Child support is the payment of money from one parent to another for the maintenance of the child or children of that relationship, whether or not the parties to the relationship were ever married. The payment of child support is usually made to the custodial parent—the parent with whom the child legally resides—by the noncustodial parent. The terms of the child support award can be agreed upon by the parties, as long as the custodial parent is made aware of the amount the child may be entitled to under the law. The agreement must be fair to all parties and in the best interests of the child. Upon application to a court, the parent can have agreement converted into an enforceable legal order. If the parties cannot agree to a support amount, then the decision will be made by the court after a formal hearing.

The payment of child support is a legal obligation which continues until either the child is emancipated or the paying parent dies. Emancipation occurs when the child reaches the age of majority, which is usually eighteen but extends until the age of twenty-one in some states. In addition, a child may be emancipated if he or she marries, joins the armed services, or otherwise voluntarily leaves the care and control of the custodial parent. However, emancipation does not necessarily occur just because a child physically leaves the custodial parent's household, such as for the purpose of attending school.

> EXAMPLE: John and Mary divorce and Mary is awarded custody of, and child support for, their 17-year-old son, John Jr. They live in New York, where the age of majority is 21. When John Jr. turns 18, he enlists in the Marines. John stops paying child support to Mary. Mary petitions the court for John to continue child support payments because John Jr. has not yet reached the age of 21.

> POSSIBLE OUTCOME: The court may rule that John Jr. has been emancipated because he joined the Marines and, therefore, John no longer is obligated to pay child support payments to Mary. However, if John Jr. is subsequently discharged from the military and returns to live with Mary

before he reaches the age of majority, John may once again be obligated to pay child support payments to Mary until John Jr. reaches the age of 21.

FEDERAL CHILD SUPPORT GUIDELINES

In 1989, the federal government enacted child support guidelines which each state is mandated to use in determining the amount of child support orders in cases where the parties cannot mutually agree to support amounts. The child support guidelines set forth a formula, based on such factors as parental income and the number of children for whom support is sought, in order to arrive at the support amount. The child support guidelines must be used unless it can be shown that to use them would be unjust or inappropriate in a particular case. If a court departs from using the guidelines in any case, it must give its reasons, on the record, for its decision.

A Child Support Worksheet is set forth at Appendix 21.

Federal/State Child Support Enforcement

The federal government requires the states to implement enforcement programs to ensure that child support is paid. The child support enforcement program is usually handled by the state's child support enforcement office in conjunction with the domestic relations or family court of the jurisdiction. The enforcement program assists the custodial parent in locating an absent, non-paying parent, establishing paternity, establishing the support order, and collecting and enforcing the child support order.

Locating an Absent Parent

The federal government has established the Federal Parent Locator Service (FPLS), which uses information contained in federal records, such as Internal Revenue Service files, Social Security files, and Veterans Administration files, to locate absent parents. In addition, each state has established a State Parent Locator Services (SPLS), which uses state records, such as Department of Motor Vehicles files and state unemployment insurance files, to locate absent parents.

Establishing Paternity

When the parents of a child were never married, the paternity of the child must be established before an order of support can be made. If the father does not object to paternity, he can sign a written admission of paternity, which can be filed with the court. However, if the father is contesting paternity, the matter must be decided by a court. Evidence, such as blood and genetic tests, will be produced to support the paternity petition. Once paternity is established, the child is legally entitled to the same rights and privileges as a child born of married parents, including the right to support, inheritance, and other benefits.

Establishing the Support Order

After the noncustodial parent is located, an enforceable support order must be established. Most states use administrative procedures to expedite the establishment of a legally binding support order. If the parties agree to the amount of support, the agreement can be made into a legally enforceable order of support as long as it conforms to certain requirements of fairness. If the parties cannot agree, a hearing is conducted to establish the terms of the support order. Depending on the laws of the particular state, support awards can be increased or decreased if one of the parties seeks modification of the order. The ability to modify a support order depends on certain factors, as set forth by the state, which may include a change in circumstances of the parties, such as a loss of employment, or a change in the needs of the child.

If the noncustodial parent is employed and covered by health insurance through his or her employer, the Court may also order the health plan administrator to enroll the unemancipated children in the health plan and provide the custodial parent with identification cards and other information necessary to access the health care coverage. A certified copy of this signed order must generally be served on the employer of the person legally responsible to provide health insurance.

A sample Qualified Medical Child Support Order is set forth at Appendix 22.

Enforcing the Support Order

In recognition of the need for strict enforcement of child support orders, the federal government has implemented a variety of rules for the collection of child support. The states are obligated to follow those directives. For example, as of January 1994, all child support orders will be subject to immediate wage withholding unless both parents and/or the court agree to a different plan. Presently, wage withholding only applies to new child support enforcement cases, or for existing cases, at the request of either parent, as long as the state agrees. A noncustodial parent can also request his or her employer to make automatic payroll deductions for child support, and the employer is required, under federal law, to comply with this request.

In certain circumstances, the court may direct that the payment of spousal support or child support be made by automatically deducting funds from the noncustodial parent's wages through the use of an Income Deduction Order. This can occur only where the paying spouse is a salaried employee. Under the order, the employer is required to deduct the support payment from the noncustodial parent's paycheck and forward it either directly to the custodial parent or to an agency responsible for collecting and disbursing the payments.

A sample Income Deduction Order is set forth at Appendix 23.

When the noncustodial parent is self-employed, or otherwise not easily subject to wage withholding, and reneges on his or her obligation to pay child support, other enforcement action can be taken. Such action may include placing liens on the real or personal property of the debtor parent or intercepting the federal or state income tax refunds of the debtor parent. In addition, child support arrears may be reported to consumer credit agencies.

States are also required to vigorously pursue the enforcement of child support orders against out-of-state noncustodial parents. Each state has its own form of interstate enforcement legislation, such as the Uniform Reciprocal Enforcement of Support Act (URESA), which provides for the enforcement of support orders across state lines.

TAX ASPECTS OF CHILD SUPPORT

Child support is not considered income to the parent who receives the payments and is not deductible from the taxable income of the paying parent. In order to claim a child as a dependent, a parent must contribute more than fifty percent of the child's total support. Generally, the custodial parent may claim the exemption. However, the parents may agree otherwise. If the custodial parent assigns the exemption, in writing, to the noncustodial parent, the noncustodial parent can claim the exemption on his or her tax return.

CHAPTER 7:
CHILD CUSTODY

A HISTORICAL OVERVIEW

Under early Roman law, the father's power over his children, and right to custody, was absolute. The father's right to custody of the children continued in Europe well into the nineteenth century until a modification in the English common law allowed custody of children under the age of seven to be given to the mother. In 1873, the law was expanded to allow mothers to retain custody.

The common law rule granting custody solely to fathers was embraced by the American colonies and continued well into the 1800's. The father had an absolute right to custody unless he was proved to be unfit. However, in the mid-nineteenth century, in a drastic turnabout, mothers were given preference in custody determinations under the so-called *Tender Years Doctrine*. This doctrine, which was adopted in virtually every state, provided for a maternal preference with respect to the custody of young children unless proven unfit. Mothers were granted custody in almost all contested custody cases. This maternal preference continued to dominate custody decisions until the 1980's, when a trend towards equal custody rights emerged, and most states eliminated the maternal preference by case law or statute.

All jurisdictions have now discarded the absolute maternal preference. Today, most jurisdictions rely on a variety of factors to decide what type of custody would be in the best interests of the child." Although there have been rapid advances towards fair and equal determinations of custody between the fathers and mothers, it should be noted that many judges still retain the notion that mothers are the better caretakers of young children, and this attitude is often reflected in their custody decisions. However, if challenged, a judge's decision to give preference to a parent on the basis of sex would most likely be held unconstitutional.

CUSTODY FOLLOWING DIVORCE

A divorce involving children is perhaps the most emotional and painful process a family can endure. The impact on the children of the divorce can be devastating. While divorce may end the role of spouse, it does not end the role of parent, although that role is drastically altered following divorce. Often, a divorce results in drastic changes in the lifestyle of a child, and these adjustments are not easily made. Great care and attention must be given to the emotional well-being of children following a divorce, and every effort should be made to amicably resolve issues of custody and visitation without having to involve the children. Children must never be used as bargaining chips in divorce negotiations. Whatever differences the adults may have with each other, the best interests of the child should always be paramount.

TYPES OF CUSTODY

There are a number of custody arrangements available to parents following a divorce. The parties must carefully determine which arrangement will work best in their own situation. If parents can amicably agree to work out child custody issues in a reasonable manner, without having to resort to litigation, the children will have a much better chance of adjusting to their new living arrangements. It is always preferable to work out a mutually agreeable solution, rather than resort to a court to force a custody decision that may cause resentment and bitterness. The three most common types of custody arrangements are sole custody, joint custody, and split custody.

Sole Custody

Sole custody exists when one parent is designated the custodial parent—i.e., the parent who takes care of the basic daily needs of the child and who is solely in charge of making all decisions concerning the child, including those decisions affecting the child's education and health, without having to consult the other parent. In a sole custody situation, the child lives with the custodial parent. Although the noncustodial parent does not relinquish parenthood, his or her role is severely limited and consists mainly of visits with the child. This is particularly difficult where the noncustodial parent was previously very involved in the child's upbringing. In such a case, in order to lessen the emotional impact of losing the daily contact with both parents that the child previously enjoyed, it is important that the noncustodial parent maintain as close a relationship with the child as possible under the circumstances.

Joint Custody

Joint custody exists when both parents legally share responsibility for the child. Although the living arrangements may be similar to that of a sole custody situation, joint custody implies that both parents are entitled to take equal responsibility for any decisions affecting the child. In joint custody arrangements, there may also be efforts to have the child's time divided more evenly between the parents. For example, the child may be in the physical custody of the mother during weekdays and in the physical custody of the father during weekends. There are a variety of ways in which living arrangements can be worked out as long as the parents are dedicated to making joint custody work.

Split Custody

In families where there is more than one child, split custody may be an alternative—i.e., each party may take custody of one or more of the children. For example, the boys may live with the father and the girls may live with the mother. The courts are not in favor of splitting up the children in a family, however, based on a general belief that it is best for children of the same family to grow up together, particularly since siblings can be a great source of stability and comfort to one another following a divorce.

CUSTODY FACTORS

In the unfortunate event that parents cannot amicably agree to a reasonable custody arrangement, the custody dispute must be settled in court. Of course, custody litigation should be avoided if at all possible, and should be reserved only for those instances where a child's welfare would be seriously endangered by living with a parent who is clearly unfit.

Although the rules vary from state to state, most courts determining child custody take into account certain factors and award custody according to the best interests of the child. The factors commonly considered include: the emotional ties between the parent and child; the mental and physical fitness of the parent; the parent's ability to provide a stable and nurturing environment for the child; the parental preference of a child who is of sufficient age and maturity; and the willingness of the proposed custodial parent to cooperate in encouraging a good relationship between the child and the noncustodial parent. In addition, courts often order home studies and psychological evaluations of both parents before making custody determinations.

A table setting forth criteria commonly used by Courts to determine custody, by state, is set forth at Appendix 24.

In many jurisdictions, the court may appoint a law guardian—an attorney for the child—who makes an impartial determination as to which parent would make the better custodian of the child. The courts have backed away from using the financial resources of either parent as a basis for awarding custody, and have instead used the child support and property distribution awards to ensure that the custodial parent has adequate means to financially support the child.

RIGHTS OF THE NONCUSTODIAL PARENT TO VISITATION

In almost all cases, the noncustodial parent has an absolute right to visitation with the child and, if the custodial parent maliciously or willfully interferes with that right, some jurisdictions will use this interference as a basis to transfer physical custody to the other parent.

> EXAMPLE: John and Mary divorce and Mary is awarded custody of their minor son, John Jr. John is awarded liberal visitation rights according to an explicit schedule, which includes every other weekend, certain holidays, Father's Day, and one half of the summer and winter vacations. John subsequently remarries, which angers Mary who has always been very jealous. Out of spite, Mary does not want John Jr. to visit John and his new wife. Every time John arrives to pick up John Jr. as scheduled, Mary comes up with an excuse why John cannot see John Jr. This goes on for several months, until John petitions the court to enforce his visitation rights. When he arrives to pick up John Jr. for his scheduled visitation during summer vacation, he finds that Mary has maliciously sent John Jr. out of state to visit her relatives. John petitions the court for custody.

> POSSIBLE OUTCOME: The court may rule that physical custody revert to John because of Mary's willful and malicious violation of John's right to visitation with his son.

Only in situations where the noncustodial parent is clearly a danger to the child will the court attempt to curtail the visitation rights of the noncustodial parent. In addition, attempts by the custodial parent to move the child out of the jurisdiction, thereby cutting off the noncustodial parent's visitation rights, will be seriously scrutinized by the court. The relationship between the noncustodial parent and the child is a very important factor in the court's determination.

Many jurisdictions require court approval before allowing the custodial parent to move the child out of the jurisdiction, and often will not allow such removal unless there is sufficient justification for the move, such as remarriage. Of course, the court cannot restrict the relocation of the custodial parent, but it can transfer custody of the child to the noncustodial parent if the custodial parent insists on relocating. If the custody agreement restricts relocation, the court will most likely uphold the terms of the agreement. The courts generally hold that continued contact with both parents is in the best interests of the child and should be maintained.

There has also been a trend among the states to allow third-party visitation following a divorce or the death of a parent. For example, grandparents may be awarded visitation rights with their grandchildren following the death of their own child. Stepparents are also being awarded visitation rights where they have formed a close bond with the stepchildren and it would be in the best interests of the children to maintain the close relationship.

A table setting forth third party visitation rights authorized by statute, by state, is set forth at Appendix 25.

PARENTAL KIDNAPPING AND FORUM SHOPPING

An overwhelming number of parents choose to flee with their children rather than allow the courts to determine custody. A parent may take the child and drop out of sight completely, causing the other parent to suffer emotional turmoil and financial expense in attempting to locate the child. Sometimes, a parent will relocate in a jurisdiction which he or she feels will render a more favorable determination than would have been made in the home state, particularly since it can be extremely difficult for the other parent to litigate custody in a distant jurisdiction.

The Uniform Child Custody Jurisdiction Act (UCCJA), which has been adopted by all states, and the Parental Kidnapping Prevention Act (PKPA) were promulgated to attempt to combat the serious problem of jurisdictional conflict and parental forum shopping in custody decisions. These model statutes set forth the requirements a particular jurisdiction must meet in order to make a custody determination when two states are involved, and require that both jurisdictions cooperate in determining the proper forum in which to resolve the custody dispute.

When the courts in the two different states are in conflict, the UCCJA and the PKPA provide that a federal court can rule as to which state is the proper forum in which to litigate custody. The federal court will not, however, decide the merits of a custody dispute. The provisions of the statutes favor awarding jurisdiction to the child's home state, thus deterring parental forum shopping and child snatching. The UCCJA and the PKPA prohibit courts from exercising jurisdiction in a custody action if another court has already been involved in the case.

Where a parent removes a child from a jurisdiction against court order or contrary to a custody agreement, the lawful custodial parent can obtain federal assistance in locating the child. In many jurisdictions, the parent who wrongfully takes the child is subject to criminal sanctions for abducting the child and interfering with custody.

CHAPTER 8:
THE UNIFORM MARRIAGE AND DIVORCE ACT

BACKGROUND

The Uniform Marriage and Divorce Act (UMDA or the Act) was promulgated in 1970 by the National Conference of Commissioners on Uniform State Laws (NCCUSL). Although the majority of the states have chosen not to adopt the Act, it has been identified as the policy vehicle supporting two important divorce law trends—the no-fault divorce and equitable distribution of property. Shortly before the Act was adopted, the State of California enacted the nation's first modern no-fault divorce law. Several years earlier, the NCCUSL had joined the divorce reform movement and endorsed no-fault divorce, a provision which was later incorporated into the UMDA.

Following the passage of California's no-fault divorce statute, and the promulgation of the Act, the concept of no-fault divorce spread rapidly throughout the states. Eight states—Arizona, Colorado, Illinois, Kentucky, Minnesota, Missouri, Montana, and Washington—adopted the main dissolution principles of the Act, at least in part, while the majority of the states eventually adopted some form of no-fault divorce statute. No state has adopted the marriage law provisions of the Act.

Although the Act has had limited application beyond the areas of divorce and property distribution, the UMDA is a comprehensive statute on family law. The Act is comprised of five distinct parts, each of which can be considered and adopted as separate pieces of legislation. Part 1 of the Act sets forth the general provisions of the Act. Part 2 of the Act concerns marriage. Part 3 of the Act governs dissolution of marriage. Part 4 concerns child custody and support. Part 5 of the Act sets forth the effective dates and the severability and repeal provisions. Each part is discussed more fully below.

PART 1—GENERAL PROVISIONS

Part 1 of the UMDA presents the purposes and goals of the Act—establishing uniformity of marriage and divorce laws among the states and removal of the traditional adversarial context of divorce and custody litigation.

PART 2—MARRIAGE

Part 2 of the UMDA proposes the simplification of state regulation of marriage and seeks to validate all marriages performed in the enacting state in accordance with its provisions. It provides for a minimum marrying age of 18, or 16 with parental or judicial consent, or under 16 with both parental consent and judicial approval. The Act also provides for a relatively short premarital waiting period of three days.

The Act eliminates most of the traditional marriage prohibitions, retaining only the prohibitions on bigamy and incest. If the impediment is removed, however, the marriage is validated as of the date of removal of the impediment. The Act also eliminates the traditional law with respect to annulment of marriage and substitutes a procedure for a declaration of invalidity upon specified grounds. Children born of a prohibited or invalid marriage are considered legitimate under the Act's provisions.

Common-law marriages are abolished under the Act. However, provision is made for registration of such marriages if they were valid at the time and place they were entered into.

PART 3—DISSOLUTION

Part 3 of the UMDA authorizes the dissolution of a marriage solely upon the ground that the marriage is irretrievably broken. All fault grounds and defenses are eliminated. If both parties to the marriage agree that the marriage is irretrievably broken, evidenced by either mutually stating that fact or by failing to deny it, the court must make such a finding. If one of the parties denies that the marriage is irretrievably broken, however, the court must consider evidence in order to render such a finding. The Act requires a proper inquiry into the possibility of reconciliation and sets forth a procedure to determine whether reconciliation is feasible.

The UMDA provides for equitable distribution of the marital property by a court. The basis for this provision is the concept that marriage should be treated as a partnership whose assets must be fairly distributed between the spousal partners at divorce, without regard to their formal ownership. As an alternative to equitable distribution of all marital property, the UMDA provides for a distinction between separate and marital property, requiring only the latter to be subject to equitable distribution. In making its determination, a court must take into account such factors as the duration of the marriage, the occupations, ages and health of the parties, and each party's contribution to the acquisition of the assets of the marriage.

The UMDA also sets forth the factors to be considered in awarding spousal maintenance and child support. The Act explicitly provides that property division, spousal maintenance, and child support decisions should be made without regard to marital fault

PART 4—CUSTODY

Part 4 of the UMDA concerns child custody and support, which are to be considered without regard to marital fault. The emphasis is on discouraging protracted litigation involving children. The provisions of the Act relating to child custody are integrated with the provisions of the Uniform Child Custody Jurisdiction Act, promulgated by the NCCUSL in 1968, which deals with jurisdiction to adjudicate a custody case when more than one state has an interest in the litigation. Once jurisdiction is established, the UMDA governs procedural aspects of custody disputes. The Act also sets forth the factors a court should consider when deciding custody, which is to be determined according to the best interests of the child.

PART 5—EFFECTIVE DATE AND REPEALER

Part 5 of the UMDA sets forth the effective dates, severability, and repeal provisions of the Act.

THE UMDA—A VALUABLE RESOURCE

Although the states have been slow to adopt the provisions set forth in the UMDA, the trend towards reform of marriage and divorce law continues. A majority of the jurisdictions have adopted no-fault divorce statutes and equitable distribution standards of property distribution. The state legislatures, in attempting to reform their laws, have used the language of the UMDA as a principal source of both policy and language. Although the Act's goal of widespread adoption by the states has not been realized, its value as a model for statutory reform should not be underestimated or overlooked.

APPENDIX 1:
STATEMENT OF CLIENT'S RIGHTS

Your attorney is providing you with this document to inform you of what you, as a client, are entitled to by law or by custom. To help prevent any misunderstanding between you and your attorney please read this document carefully.

If you ever have any questions about these rights, or about the way your case is being handled, do not hesitate to ask your attorney. He or she should be readily available to represent your best interests and keep you informed about your case.

An attorney may not refuse to represent you on the basis of race, creed, color, sex, sexual orientation, age, national origin or disability.

You are entitled to an attorney who will be capable of handling your case; show you courtesy and consideration at all times; represent you zealously; and preserve your confidences and secrets that are revealed in the course of the relationship.

You are entitled to a written retainer agreement which must set forth, in plain language, the nature of the relationship and the details of the fee arrangement. At your request, and before you sign the agreement, you are entitled to have your attorney clarify in writing any of its terms, or include additional provisions.

You are entitled to fully understand the proposed rates and retainer fee before you sign a retainer agreement, as in any other contract.

You may refuse to enter into any fee arrangement that you find unsatisfactory.

Your attorney may not request a fee that is contingent on the securing of a divorce or on the amount of money or property that may be obtained.

Your attorney may not request a retainer fee that is nonrefundable. That is, should you discharge your attorney, or should your attorney withdraw from the case, before the retainer is used up, he or she is entitled to be paid commensurate with the work performed on your case and any expenses, but must return the balance of the retainer to you. However, your attorney may enter into a minimum fee arrangement with you that provides for the payment of a specific amount below which the fee will not fall based upon the handling of the case to its conclusion.

You are entitled to know the approximate number of attorneys and other legal staff members who will be working on your case at any given time and what you will be charged for the services of each.

You are entitled to know in advance how you will be asked to pay legal fees and expenses, and how the retainer, if any, will be spent.

At your request, and after your attorney has had a reasonable opportunity to investigate your case, you are entitled to be given an estimate of approximate future costs of your case, which estimate shall be made in good faith but may be subject to change due to facts and circumstances affecting the case.

You are entitled to receive a written, itemized bill on a regular basis, at least every 60 days.

You are expected to review the itemized bills sent by counsel, and to raise any objections or errors in a timely manner. Time spent in discussion or explanation of bills will not be charged to you.

You are expected to be truthful in all discussions with your attorney, and to provide all relevant information and documentation to enable him or her to competently prepare your case.

You are entitled to be kept informed of the status of your case, and to be provided with copies of correspondence and documents prepared on your behalf or received from the court or your adversary.

You have the right to be present in court at the time that conferences are held.

You are entitled to make the ultimate decision on the objectives to be pursued in your case, and to make the final decision regarding the settlement of your case.

Your attorney's written retainer agreement must specify under what circumstances he or she might seek to withdraw as your attorney for nonpayment of legal fees. If an action or proceeding is pending, the court may give your attorney a "charging lien," which entitles your attorney to payment for services already rendered at the end of the case out of the proceeds of the final order or judgment.

You are under no legal obligation to sign a confession of judgment or promissory note, or to agree to a lien or mortgage on your home to cover legal fees. Your attorney's written retainer agreement must specify whether, and under what circumstances, such security may be requested. In no event may such security interest be obtained by your attorney without prior court approval and notice to your adversary. An attorney's security interest in the marital residence cannot be foreclosed against you.

You are entitled to have your attorney's best efforts exerted on your behalf, but no particular results can be guaranteed.

If you entrust money with an attorney for an escrow deposit in your case, the attorney must safeguard the escrow in a special bank account. You are entitled to a written escrow agreement, a written receipt, and a complete record concerning the escrow. When the terms of the escrow agreement have been performed, the attorney must promptly make payment of the escrow to all persons who are entitled to it.

In the event of a fee dispute, you may have the right to seek arbitration. Your attorney will provide you with the necessary information regarding arbitration in the event of a fee dispute, or upon your request.

Date:_____

Receipt Acknowledged:

By:_____

Signature Line—Attorney

By:_____

Signature Line—Client

Source: New York State Unified Court System.

APPENDIX 2:
STATEMENT OF CLIENT'S
RESPONSIBILITIES

Reciprocal trust, courtesy and respect are the hallmarks of the attorney-client relationship. Within that relationship, the client looks to the attorney for expertise, education, sound judgment, protection, advocacy and representation. These expectations can be achieved only if the client fulfills the following responsibilities:

1. The client is expected to treat the lawyer and the lawyer's staff with courtesy and consideration.

2. The client's relationship with the lawyer must be one of complete candor and the lawyer must be apprised of all facts or circumstances of the matter being handled by the lawyer even if the client believes that those facts may be detrimental to the client's cause or unflattering to the client.

3. The client must honor the fee arrangement as agreed to with the lawyer, in accordance with law.

4. All bills for services rendered which are tendered to the client pursuant to the agreed upon fee arrangement should be paid promptly.

5. The client may withdraw from the attorney-client relationship, subject to financial commitments under the agreed to fee arrangement, and, in certain circumstances, subject to court approval.

6. Although the client should expect that his or her correspondence, telephone calls and other communications will be answered within a reasonable time frame, the client should recognize that the lawyer has other clients equally demanding of the lawyer's time and attention.

7. The client should maintain contact with the lawyer, promptly notify the lawyer of any change in telephone number or address and respond promptly to a request by the lawyer for information and cooperation.

---

8. The client must realize that the lawyer need respect only legitimate objectives of the client and that the lawyer will not advocate or propose positions which are unprofessional or contrary to law or the Lawyer's Code of Professional Responsibility.

9. The lawyer may be unable to accept a case if the lawyer has previous professional commitments which will result in inadequate time being available for the proper representation of a new client.

10. A lawyer is under no obligation to accept a client if the lawyer determines that the cause of the client is without merit, a conflict of interest would exist or that a suitable working relationship with the client is not likely.[1]

---

1   Source: New York State Unified Court System.

APPENDIX 3:
MARRIAGE STATUTES—AGE REQUIREMENTS

JURISDICTION	AGE WITH PARENTAL CONSENT		AGE WITHOUT PARENTAL CONSENT	
	Male	Female	Male	Female
Alabama	14	14	18	18
Alaska	16	16	18	18
Arizona	16	16	18	18
Arkansas	17	16	18	18
California	None	None	18	18
Colorado	16	16	18	18
Connecticut	16	16	18	18
Delaware	18	16	18	18
District of Columbia	16	16	18	18
Florida	16	16	18	18
Georgia	16	16	18	18
Hawaii	15	15	18	18
Idaho	16	16	18	18
Illinois	16	16	18	18
Indiana	17	17	18	18
Iowa	16	16	18	18
Kansas	14	12	18	18

JURISDICTION	AGE WITH PARENTAL CONSENT		AGE WITHOUT PARENTAL CONSENT	
Kentucky	18	18	18	18
Louisiana	18	18	18	18
Maine	16	16	18	18
Maryland	16	16	18	18
Massachusetts	14	12	18	18
Michigan	16	16	18	18
Minnesota	16	16	18	18
Mississippi	None	None	17	15
Missouri	15	15	18	18
Montana	16	16	18	18
Nebraska	17	17	19	19
Nevada	16	16	18	18
New Hampshire	14	13	18	18
New Jersey	16	16	18	18
New Mexico	16	16	18	18
New York	16	16	18	18
North Carolina	16	16	18	18
North Dakota	16	16	18	18
Ohio	18	16	18	18
Oklahoma	16	16	18	18
Oregon	17	17	18	18
Pennsylvania	16	16	18	18
Rhode Island	18	16	18	18
South Carolina	16	14	18	18
South Dakota	16	16	18	18
Tennessee	16	16	18	18
Texas	14	14	18	18
Utah	14	14	18	18

JURISDICTION	AGE WITH PARENTAL CONSENT		AGE WITHOUT PARENTAL CONSENT	
Vermont	16	16	18	18
Virginia	16	16	18	18
Washington	17	17	18	18
West Virginia	18	18	18	18
Wisconsin	16	16	18	18
Wyoming	16	16	18	18

In Alabama, Florida, Utah, Virginia and the District of Columbia, parental consent is not required if the minor was previously married.

In Arkansas, Delaware, Florida, Georgia, Indiana, Maryland, New Jersey, New Mexico, North Carolina, Ohio, Oklahoma, South Carolina, South Dakota, Virginia, and West Virginia, there is a statutory procedure whereby younger parties may obtain a license in case of pregnancy or birth of child.

In Alaska, Arizona, Arkansas, Colorado, Connecticut, Idaho, Louisiana, Maine, Nevada, New Jersey, Ohio, and Oklahoma, younger parties may marry with parental consent and permission of the court, or in some cases with judicial consent alone.

In Texas, parental consent and permission of the court is required below age 18.[1]

---

1   Source: Legal Information Institute.

APPENDIX 4:
MARRIAGE STATUTES—STATUTORY

WAITING PERIOD BEFORE ISSUANCE OF LICENSE

JURISDICTION	WAITING PERIOD
Alabama	None
Alaska	3 days (may be avoided)
Arizona	None
Arkansas	None but parties must file notice of intention to marry with local clerk
California	None
Colorado	None
Connecticut	None (may be avoided)
Delaware	24 hours
District of Columbia	3 days (may be avoided)
Florida	None
Georgia	3 days unless parties or 18 years of age or more; female is pregnant; or applicants are the parents of a living child born out of wedlock
Hawaii	None
Idaho	None
Illinois	1 day
Indiana	None
Iowa	3 days
Kansas	3 days (may be avoided)
Kentucky	None

JURISDICTION	WAITING PERIOD
Louisiana	None
Maine	3 days (may be avoided); parties must file notice of intention to marry with local clerk
Maryland	48 hours (may be avoided)
Massachusetts	3 days; parties must file notice of intention to marry with local clerk
Michigan	3 days (may be avoided)
Minnesota	5 days (may be avoided)
Mississippi	3 days (may be avoided)
Missouri	None
Montana	None
Nebraska	None
Nevada	None
New Hampshire	3 days (may be avoided); parties must file notice of intention to marry with local clerk
New Jersey	72 hours (may be avoided)
New Mexico	None
New York	24 hours
North Carolina	None
North Dakota	None
Ohio	5 days (may be avoided); applicants under age 18 must state that they have had marriage counseling
Oklahoma	3 days if one or both parties are below the age for marriage without parental consent
Oregon	3 days (may be avoided)
Pennsylvania	3 days (may be avoided)
Rhode Island	None
South Carolina	1 day
South Dakota	None
Tennessee	3 days unless parties are over the age of 18 (may be avoided)

JURISDICTION	WAITING PERIOD
Texas	72 hours
Utah	None
Vermont	1 day (may be avoided)
Virginia	None
Washington	3 days
West Virginia	3 days (may be avoided)
Wisconsin	5 days (may be avoided)
Wyoming	None[1]

---

1   Source: Legal Information Institute.

APPENDIX 5:
MARRIAGE STATUTES—DURATION OF
LICENSE VALIDITY

JURISDICTION	DURATION
Alabama	30 days
Alaska	3 months
Arizona	1 year
Arkansas	No expiration
California	90 days
Colorado	30 days
Connecticut	65 days
Delaware	30 days
District of Columbia	No expiration
Florida	60 days
Georgia	30 days
Hawaii	30 days
Idaho	No expiration
Illinois	60 days
Indiana	60 days
Iowa	20 days
Kansas	6 months
Kentucky	30 days
Louisiana	No expiration

JURISDICTION	DURATION
Maine	90 days
Maryland	6 months
Massachusetts	60 days
Michigan	33 days
Minnesota	6 months
Mississippi	No expiration
Missouri	30 days
Montana	180 days
Nebraska	1 year
Nevada	1 year
New Hampshire	90 days
New Jersey	30 days
New Mexico	No expiration
New York	60 days
North Carolina	No expiration
North Dakota	60 days
Ohio	60 days
Oklahoma	30 days
Oregon	60 days
Pennsylvania	60 days
Rhode Island	3 months
South Carolina	No expiration
South Dakota	20 days
Tennessee	30 days
Texas	30 days
Utah	30 days
Vermont	No expiration
Virginia	60 days
Washington	60 days

JURISDICTION	DURATION
West Virginia	No expiration
Wisconsin	30 days
Wyoming	No expiration[1]

---

1   Source: Legal Information Institute.

APPENDIX 6:
MARRIAGE STATUTES—COMMON-LAW MARRIAGE

JURISDICTION	COMMON-LAW MARRIAGE RECOGNIZED
Alabama	Yes
Alaska	No unless entered into before 1917
Arizona	No unless valid where contracted
Arkansas	No unless valid where contracted
California	No unless entered into before 1895 or if valid where contracted
Colorado	Yes
Connecticut	No unless valid where contracted
Delaware	No unless valid where contracted
District of Columbia	Yes
Florida	No unless entered into before 1/1/68 or if valid where contracted
Georgia	No unless entered into prior to 1/1/97
Hawaii	No unless valid where contracted
Idaho	No unless entered into prior to 1/1/97
Illinois	No
Indiana	No unless entered into before 1/1/58
Iowa	Yes
Kansas	Yes
Kentucky	No unless valid where contracted

JURISDICTION	COMMON-LAW MARRIAGE RECOGNIZED
Louisiana	No unless valid where contracted
Maine	No unless valid where contracted
Maryland	No unless valid where contracted
Massachusetts	No unless valid where contracted
Michigan	No unless entered into before 1/1/57 or if valid where contracted
Minnesota	No unless entered into before 4/26/41 or if valid where contracted
Mississippi	No unless entered into before 4/5/56
Missouri	No unless entered into before 3/31/21 or if valid where contracted
Montana	Yes
Nebraska	No unless entered into before 1/1/23 or if valid where contracted
Nevada	No unless entered into before 3/29/33 or if valid where contracted
New Hampshire	No unless valid where contracted
New Jersey	No unless entered into before 12/1/39 or if valid where contracted
New Mexico	No unless valid where contracted
New York	No unless entered into before 4/29/33 or if valid where contracted
North Carolina	No unless valid where contracted
North Dakota	No unless valid where contracted
Ohio	No
Oklahoma	Yes
Oregon	No unless valid where contracted
Pennsylvania	Yes
Rhode Island	Yes
South Carolina	Yes
South Dakota	No unless entered into before 1959 or if valid where contracted

JURISDICTION	COMMON-LAW MARRIAGE RECOGNIZED
Tennessee	No unless valid where contracted
Texas	Yes
Utah	Yes
Vermont	No unless valid where contracted
Virginia	No unless valid where contracted
Washington	No unless valid where contracted
West Virginia	No unless valid where contracted
Wisconsin	No unless valid where contracted
Wyoming	No unless valid where contracted[1]

---

1   Source: Legal Information Institute.

APPENDIX 7:
SAMPLE PRENUPTIAL AGREEMENT

This Prenuptial Agreement is made and entered into this *[Insert Date of Agreement]*, in the City of *[Name of City]*, State of *[Name of State]*, by and between *[Name]* residing at *[Address]*, (hereinafter "Husband") and *[Name]*, residing at *[Address]*, (hereinafter "Wife").

W I T N E S S E T H :

WHEREAS, the parties to this agreement are unmarried persons who are considering entering into a ceremonial marriage on or about *[Insert Date of Intended Marriage]*, in the *[Name of City]*, *[Name of State]*.

WHEREAS, each of the parties has [not] been previously married. *[Note: If either or both parties have been previously married, provide details, including names and dates of birth of any children of the previous marriage]*.

WHEREAS, in anticipation of this marriage, the parties desire to confirm, by this agreement, the rights and obligations which will accrue to them, by reason of this marriage, and to accept the provisions of this agreement, in settlement of all rights and claims arising out of this marriage.

WHEREAS, each party agrees that they have had the opportunity to fully discuss this agreement between themselves and with counsel of their own choosing. This discussion included full disclosure of all property owned by each party, each party's liabilities and income, and all other matters pertaining to their respective financial circumstances. A copy of a schedule containing financial circumstances of each party is attached hereto as Exhibit A and B, respectively.

NOW, THEREFORE, in consideration of the mutual covenants herein, the parties agree as follows:

1. **Consideration**: The consideration for this agreement is based upon the mutual promises and waivers herein contained, and the marriage which is to be solemnized. If the marriage does not take place, this agreement shall be deemed null and void for all purposes.

2. **Separate Property**: The parties agree to keep, as their separate property, all of their respective premarital property and any property subsequently acquired by gift or inheritance, including any increase of such property and any property acquired in exchange for such property.

3. **Marital Property**: The parties intend that any assets acquired by each or both of them during their marriage, which are not contained in Exhibits A and B of this Agreement, will be considered marital property, and subject to division as marital property.

4. **Waivers**: If this marriage is terminated by death, or dissolved by legal proceedings, each party hereby waives any rights to alimony, maintenance or spousal support of any kind; to dower or curtesy or homestead rights; and to any statutory rights in the other's estate except for those rights to marital property reserved under paragraph 3 above.

5. **Testamentary Provisions**: Notwithstanding the provisions of paragraph 4 above, the parties agree that nothing herein shall be construed to prevent either party from naming the other as a beneficiary of his or her will, or as a donee through gift. However, this paragraph should not be construed as requiring either party to make a gift or a provision in his or her will for the other party.

6. **Additional Instruments**: Each party shall take any and all steps and execute and deliver any and all instruments and documents which may be reasonably required for the purpose of giving full force and effect to the provisions of this Agreement.

7. **Waiver of Strict Performance**: This Agreement constitutes the entire understanding of the parties and no modification or waiver of its terms shall be valid unless in writing and signed by the parties. This Agreement shall not be subject to modification by any court of law. No waiver of a breach or default of any provision of this Agreement shall be deemed a waiver of any subsequent breach or default.

8. **Binding Effect**: This Agreement shall be binding upon the parties, the heirs, personal representatives and assigns.

9. **Partial Invalidity**: In the event that any provision of this Agreement is held to be illegal, invalid, unenforceable, or against public policy, the remaining provisions of the Agreement shall remain valid and enforceable.

10. **Situs**: This Agreement shall be subject to the law of the State of *[Name of State]*, the residence of *[husband/wife]*. *[Note: The resi-*

dence of one of the parties to the agreement should be chosen as the state whose law shall apply in case of a dispute].

11. **Social Security Numbers**: The Social Security Number of the Husband is *[Insert SS#]*. The Social Security Number of the Wife is *[Insert SS#]*.

12. **Attorneys**: The attorney for the Husband is *[Name of Attorney]*, with offices located at *[Address of Attorney]*. The attorney for the Wife is *[Name of Attorney]*, with offices located at *[Address of Attorney]*.

13. **Entire Agreement**: This Agreement contains the entire understanding of the parties, and there are no representations, warranties, covenants or undertakings other than those expressly set forth herein.

IN WITNESS WHEREOF, the parties hereto have set their hands and seals the day and year first written above.

_____

Signature Line—Wife

_____

Signature Line—Husband

STATE OF

COUNTY OF

On the _____ day of _____, 2001, before me personally came *[Name of Husband and Name of Wife]*, to me known and known to me to be the individuals described in and who executed the foregoing Agreement, and they acknowledged to me that they executed the same.

Notary Public Stamp and Signature

APPENDIX 8:
SAMPLE COHABITATION AGREEMENT

This Agreement is made and entered into this *[Insert Date of Agreement]*, in the City of *[Name of City]*, State of *[Name of State]*, by and between *[Name of Partner #1]* residing at *[Address]*, and *[Name of Partner #2]*, residing at *[Address]*.

WITNESSETH:

WHEREAS, the parties to this agreement are unmarried persons who began cohabiting *[or who intend to cohabit with each other]* on or about *[Insert Date]*, in the *[Name of City]*, *[Name of State]*. The parties contemplate that this relationship will continue indefinitely, unless terminated as set forth herein.

WHEREAS, the parties declare at this time that they do not intend to become married to each other. Nevertheless, in the event that the parties do marry, it is their mutual intent that this Agreement be deemed a prenuptial agreement and that its terms be given full force and effect as such. Notwithstanding the foregoing, the parties do not intend this cohabitation to be deemed the creation of a common law marriage in any jurisdiction whatsoever.

WHEREAS, in anticipation of their cohabitation, the parties desire to confirm, by this Agreement, the responsibilities, rights and obligations which each party has declared for the other, to establish ownership rights of separate property of the parties; to provide for partnership property; and to provide for any and all other financial and legal consequences arising out of this cohabitation.

WHEREAS, each party agrees that they have had the opportunity to fully discuss this Agreement between themselves and with counsel of their own choosing. This discussion included full disclosure of all property owned by each party, each party's liabilities and income, and all other matters pertaining to their respective financial circumstances. A copy of a schedule containing financial circumstances of each party is attached hereto as Exhibit A and B, respectively.

NOW, THEREFORE, in consideration of the mutual covenants herein, the parties agree as follows:

1. *Consideration:* The consideration for this agreement is based upon the mutual promises and waivers herein contained. If the co-habitation intended by this Agreement fails to take place, this Agreement shall be deemed null and void for all purposes. *[Note: It is important to understand that an agreement founded solely on a meretricious relationship may be deemed void as against public policy and it is thus important to base this Agreement on the contractual provisions each party is providing the other, based on partnership principles].*

2. *Separate Property:* The parties agree to keep, as their separate property, all of their respective property as set forth on Exhibits A and B of this Agreement, and that any property subsequently acquired by gift or inheritance, including any increase of such property and any property acquired in exchange for such property, shall remain separate property.

3. *Joint Property:* The parties agree that from time to time they may voluntarily acquire joint assets, but no property shall be deemed a joint asset unless it is so designated by the parties, in writing, at the time the joint property is acquired. The writing shall indicate the percentage of interest retained by each party in the joint asset.

4. *Income and Expenses:* The parties intend that the income of each party shall be shared as joint income of the parties *[or shall be the separate property of the party earning such income].* During the term of their cohabitation, the parties agree to share all living expenses as follows: *[Note: The parties may set forth the specific terms of their arrangement as it pertains to the payment of expenses, the expenses which are considered joint expenses and the expenses which shall remain separate expenses of the parties].*

5. *Support:* Each party agrees that neither party shall seek support from the other and each hereby waives any right of support of any kind from the other party subsequent to separation or death of the other party. *[Note: The parties may alternatively agree to a schedule of support of either party, particularly in situations where one party is gainfully employed while assisting the other party with furtherance of his or her education during the period of cohabitation].*

6. *Testamentary Provisions:* Notwithstanding the foregoing, the parties agree that nothing herein shall be construed to prevent either party from naming the other as a beneficiary of his or her will, or as a donee through gift. However, this paragraph should not be con-

strued as requiring either party to make a gift or a provision in his or her will for the other party.

7. *Specific Responsibilities:* The parties intend by this Agreement to share living expenses and household chores on a fair and cooperative basis. *[Note: The parties can provide the specific details of their arrangement in as much detail as desired, however, it should be noted that courts generally will not uphold provisions relating to specific performance of personal services, such as the performance of household chores].*

8. *Birth Control:* The parties mutually agree to practice birth control by such methods as may be determined by the parties in consultation with their respective physicians. In the event that notwithstanding the foregoing, a pregnancy shall occur, the decision as to whether the child shall be aborted or born shall be the joint decision of both parties *[or the sole decision of the mother, etc.]*.

9. *Children:* In the event a child is born of this relationship, both parents agree to recognize the child as their legitimate child and agree to assume joint parental responsibility for its support. It is further agreed that the parties shall have joint custody of said child.

10. *Cessation of Cohabitation:* The cohabitation of the parties may be terminated at any time by either party, in which case each party shall retain his or her own separate property as set forth herein, and the joint property shall be divided on the basis of contribution of each party to said asset as set forth in paragraph 3 above.

11. *Waiver of Strict Performance:* This Agreement constitutes the entire understanding of the parties and no modification or waiver of its terms shall be valid unless in writing and signed by the parties. This Agreement shall not be subject to modification by any court of law. No waiver of a breach or default of any provision of this Agreement shall be deemed a waiver of any subsequent breach or default.

12. *Binding Effect:* This Agreement shall be binding upon the parties, the heirs, personal representatives and assigns.

13. *Partial Invalidity:* In the event that any provision of this Agreement is held to be illegal, invalid, unenforceable, or against public policy, the remaining provisions of the Agreement shall remain valid and enforceable.

14. *Situs:* This Agreement shall be subject to the law of the State of *[Name of State]*, the residence of *[Partner #1/Partner #2]*. *[Note: The residence of one of the parties to the agreement should be chosen as the state whose law shall apply in case of a dispute].*

15. *Social Security Numbers:* The Social Security Number of the parties are as follows: *[Set forth the respective social security numbers of the parties].*

16. *Attorneys: [Set forth the names and addresses of the attorneys for the parties, if any].*

17. *Entire Agreement:* This Agreement contains the entire understanding of the parties, and there are no representations, warranties, covenants or undertakings other than those expressly set forth herein.

IN WITNESS WHEREOF, the parties hereto have set their hands and seals the day and year first written above.

_____

Signature Line—Partner #1

_____

Signature Line—Partner #2

STATE OF

COUNTY OF

On the _____ day of _____, 2001, before me personally came *[Name of Partner #1 and Name of Partner #2]*, to me known and known to me to be the individuals described in and who executed the foregoing Agreement, and they acknowledged to me that they executed the same.

Notary Public Stamp and Signature

APPENDIX 9:
STATES THAT PREVENT RECOGNITION OF OUT-OF-STATE SAME-SEX MARRIAGE LICENSE BY STATUTE

JURISDICTION	YEAR LAW PASSED
Alabama	1998
Alaska	1998
Arizona	1996
Arkansas	1997
California	2000
Colorado	2000
Delaware	1996
Florida	1997
Georgia	1996
Hawaii	1998
Idaho	1996
Illinois	1996
Indiana	1997
Iowa	1998
Kansas	1996
Kentucky	1998
Louisiana	1999
Maine	1997

STATES THAT PREVENT RECOGNITION OF OUT-OF-STATE SAME-SEX MARRIAGE LICENSE BY STATUTE

JURISDICTION	YEAR LAW PASSED
Michigan	1996
Minnesota	1997
Mississippi	1997
Missouri	2001
Montana	1997
Nebraska	2000
North Carolina	1996
North Dakota	1997
Oklahoma	1996
Pennsylvania	1996
South Carolina	1996
South Dakota	1996
Tennessee	1996
Utah	1995
Virginia	1997
Washington	1998
West Virginia	2000

APPENDIX 10:
STATES THAT DO NOT HAVE LAWS PREVENTING RECOGNITION OF OUT-OF-STATE SAME-SEX MARRIAGE LICENSE

JURISDICTION

Connecticut

Maryland

Massachusetts

Nevada

New Hampshire

New Jersey

New Mexico

New York

Ohio

Oregon

Rhode Island

Texas

Vermont

Wisconsin

Wyoming

APPENDIX 11:
SAMPLE SEPARATION
AGREEMENT—SIMPLE FORM
(NO CHILDREN)

This Agreement is made and entered into this *[Insert Date of Agreement]*, in the City of *[Name of City]*, State of *[Name of State]*, by and between *[Name]* residing at *[Address]*, (hereinafter "Husband") and *[Name]*, residing at *[Address]*, (hereinafter "Wife").

WITNESSETH:

WHEREAS, the parties to this agreement were duly married to each other on [Insert Date of Marriage], in the City of *[Name of City]*, State of *[Name of State]*.

WHEREAS, there are no issue of the said marriage and no expected issue; and

WHEREAS, certain unhappy and irreconcilable differences have arisen between the parties as a result of which they have separated and are now living separate and apart from each other; and

WHEREAS, the parties desire to confirm their separation and to resolve by agreement all issues and disputes existing between them and to settle and resolve all aspects of their respective marital rights and obligations, including but not limited to property, support, maintenance, and counsel fees, as permitted by *[the applicable state's domestic relations statutes]*.

WHEREAS, the Wife is represented by an attorney of her own selection, *[Insert Attorney's Address]*, who has offices located at *[Insert Attorney's Address]*; and the Husband is represented by an attorney of his own selection, *[Insert Attorney's Address]*, who has offices located at *[Insert Attorney's Address]*; and each of the said parties having been fully informed by his or her counsel of all legal rights and responsibilities and each fully understanding same and the terms and conditions set forth in this Agreement;

NOW, THEREFORE, in consideration of the premises and mutual covenants and undertakings hereinafter set forth, the parties agree as follows:

ARTICLE I—SEPARATION

1. It is, and shall be, lawful for the parties hereto at all times to live separate and apart from each other and to reside from time to time at such place or places as each of the parties may see fit, and to contract, carry on and engage in any employment, business, or trade, which either may deem fit, free from control, restraints, or interference, direct or indirect, by the other in all respects, as if such parties were sole and unmarried.

2. Neither of the parties shall interfere with the other or with his or her respective liberty of action or conduct, and each agrees that the other may, at any time and at all times, reside and be in such place or places and with such relatives, friends, and acquaintances, as he or she may choose, and each party agrees that he or she will not molest the other or compel or seek to compel the other party to cohabit or dwell with him or her or institute any proceedings for the restoration of conjugal right, or sue, molest, or trouble any other person for receiving, entertaining, or harboring the other party hereto. Neither party shall directly or indirectly make any statements to each other or to any other persons, which are derogatory of the other party.

ARTICLE II—MARITAL RESIDENCE

1. The parties acknowledge and agree that the marital residence was, and the Wife's primary residence remains, the cooperative apartment located at *[Insert Address of Marital Residence]*. The parties further acknowledge and agree that the Wife is the sole owner of, and holds title to, the Marital Residence, and is the sole tenant on a proprietary lease issued with respect to the Marital Residence.

2. The Wife agrees and warrants that she alone shall be responsible for the care, upkeep, maintenance, mortgage, carrying charges, assessments, and all expenses of every kind and nature in connection with the Marital Residence, including without limitation all payments and obligations with respect to any existing Cooperative loan and any and all obligations or expenses with respect to taxes, water and sewer charges, insurance, utilities, telephone, repairs and maintenance.

ARTICLE III—PERSONAL PROPERTY, BANK ACCOUNTS, HOUSEHOLD EFFECTS

The parties, having considered the circumstances of their marriage, and the facts set forth in *[the applicable State's property distribution statutes]*, hereby agree as follows with respect to the division of their marital and personal property, other than realty, including all property presently held in the name of the Husband, all property presently held in the name of the Wife, and all property presently held by either the Husband or the Wife in conjunction with any other person(s), including the Husband and the Wife:

1. The Husband and Wife acknowledge and agree that they have heretofore divided between themselves all items of furniture, furnishings and household effects, formerly or presently located in the Marital Residence.

2. The parties acknowledge and agree that as of the date of this Agreement, there exist no bank, savings, or checking accounts in their joint names. The parties further agree that henceforth they will each maintain such bank accounts as they desire in their own individual names, as separate property, and each shall make no claims upon any account held by the other.

3. The Wife shall have exclusive right, title and interest in her personal clothing and effects, including jewelry, if any. The Husband hereby waives and relinquishes any and all claims to any of the personal property described in this Paragraph and agrees to waive and release any and all claims against the Wife for any interest, of any kind or nature, in any and all property not specifically reserved to the Husband under this Agreement.

4. The Husband shall have exclusive right, title and interest in his personal clothing and effects, including jewelry, if any. The Wife hereby waives and relinquishes any and all claims to any of the personal property described in this Paragraph and agrees to waive and release any and all claims against the Husband for any interest, of any kind or nature, in any and all property not specifically reserved to the Wife under this Agreement.

ARTICLE IV—MAINTENANCE, ALIMONY AND SUPPORT

The parties, having considered their respective financial circumstances, their respective present and future earning capacities, and the relevant factors for spousal support set forth in *[the applicable State's domestic relations statutes]*, hereby agree as follows with respect to alimony, maintenance and support:

1. The Husband neither seeks nor requires any alimony, maintenance or support for himself from the Wife and, therefore, no provision for alimony, maintenance or support for the Husband is made herein. The Husband agrees that he has not claimed, and that he will not hereafter claim against the Wife for support and maintenance. The Husband hereby expressly waives and releases any and all claims to alimony, maintenance or support from the Wife.

2. The Wife neither seeks nor requires any alimony, maintenance or support for herself from the Husband and, therefore, no provision for alimony, maintenance or support for the Wife is made herein. The Wife agrees that she has not claimed, and that she will not hereafter claim against the Husband for support and maintenance. The Wife hereby expressly waives and releases any and all claims to alimony, maintenance or support from the Husband.

ARTICLE V—INSURANCE

Neither party shall be under any obligation to provide for the other any policy of health insurance, life insurance, or any other form or type of insurance.

ARTICLE VI—INCOME TAXES

1. The parties acknowledge that they have heretofore filed joint income tax returns with the appropriate federal and state taxing authorities. Except as otherwise provided herein, all liabilities on any such joint income tax returns shall be equally borne by the parties, and all refunds on such returns shall be equally divided by the parties. The Husband and Wife each hereby warrant and represent to the other that to the best of his or her knowledge all federal, state and local income tax returns on all joint returns heretofore filed by the parties have been paid, and that no interest or penalty is due with respect thereto, and that no tax deficiency proceeding is pending or threatened thereon. In the event that any claim is made or liability imposed on account of additional tax, interest or penalty or adjustment arising out of any joint return heretofore filed, which liability is attributable to understated income and/or overstated deductions of one of the parties hereto, which was not known to the other, then such claim or liability shall be the responsibility of the party whose understated income or overstated deductions resulted in the claim or liability and that party hereby agrees to indemnify and hold the other party harmless from any loss, expense (including

reasonable attorney's fees and disbursements) and damage on account thereof.

2. The parties hereby agree that they will file separate income tax returns for the year 2001 and for any subsequent year during which the parties shall remain married to each other.

3. The parties further agree that they will cooperate with each other in the event that any audit, claim, tax deficiency or other proceeding is brought by the relevant taxing authorities against the parties, or either of them, on account of any joint return heretofore filed. The parties further agree that the costs and expenses of defending such a proceeding shall be equally borne by the parties.

ARTICLE VII—DEBTS

1. The Wife assumes and henceforth will be solely responsible for the following joint debts of both parties: *[Provide details]*.

2. The Husband assumes and henceforth will be solely responsible for the following joint debts of both parties: *[Provide details]*.

3. Except as otherwise expressly stated herein, the Wife represents, warrants and covenants that she has not heretofore, nor will she hereafter, incur or contract any debt, charge, obligation or liability whatsoever for which the Husband, his legal representatives, or his property or estate is, or may become, liable. The Wife agrees to indemnify and hold the Husband harmless from all loss, expense (including reasonable attorney's fees) and damages in connection with or arising out of a breach by the Wife of her foregoing representation, warranty and covenant.

4. Except as otherwise expressly stated herein, the Husband represents, warrants and covenants that he has not heretofore, nor will he hereafter, incur or contract any debt, charge, obligation or liability whatsoever for which the Wife, her legal representatives, or her property or estate is, or may become, liable. The Husband agrees to indemnify and hold the Wife harmless from all loss, expense (including reasonable attorney's fees) and damages in connection with or arising out of a breach by the Husband of his foregoing representation, warranty and covenant.

ARTICLE VIII—INDEPENDENT REPRESENTATION

1. The parties hereto acknowledge that the Wife has been represented by *[Insert Attorney's Address]*, who has offices located at *[Insert Attorney's Address]*, an attorney of the Wife's own choosing, and that said

attorney has prepared this Agreement based upon the terms and conditions agreed to by the parties as the result of direct negotiations between them. The Husband hereby acknowledges that he has been afforded ample opportunity to study and review the provisions of this Agreement and, in connection with his review of this Agreement, has consulted with *[Insert Attorney's Address]*, who has offices located at *[Insert Attorney's Address]*, an attorney of his own choosing, and has had said attorney advise him with respect thereto. Further, the parties acknowledge that certain revisions and changes have been made as a result of discussions between the attorneys and the parties.

2. Each party shall be solely responsible for the payment of his or her own attorney's fees for services rendered in connection with the negotiation, preparation, and review of this Agreement and the matrimonial issues and disputes that have previously arisen between the parties.

3. Each party shall be solely responsible for the payment of his or her own attorney's fees for services rendered in connection with any matrimonial action which may hereafter be brought by one of the parties hereto against the other party hereto.

4. Each of the parties hereby warrants and represents to the other that he or she has dealt with no other attorney(s) for whose services the other is or may become liable and agrees to indemnify and hold the other harmless of all loss, expenses (including reasonable attorney's fees and disbursements) and damages in the event of a breach by a party of such representation and warranty. However, notwithstanding anything in this Article to the contrary, in the event that either party shall default in any of his or her obligations under this Agreement, or if he or she shall challenge unsuccessfully the validity of this Agreement or its interpretation, then that party shall be liable for the cost and expenses of the other party as a result thereof, including but not limited to, reasonable attorney's fees and disbursements.

ARTICLE IX—MUTUAL RELEASES

1. Except as otherwise expressly provided herein, each party hereby releases, remises, and forever discharges the other of and from any and all causes of action, claims, rights, or demands, whatsoever, in law or in equity, which either of the parties hereto ever had, or now has, against the other, except (a) nothing herein contained shall be deemed to prevent either party from enforcing the terms of this Agreement or from asserting such claims as are reserved by this Agreement to each party against the other or the estate of the other; provided, however, that the claims so asserted arise out of a breach of this Agreement; and (b) nothing herein contained shall impair or waive or release any and all causes

of action for a divorce, annulment, or separation or any defenses which either may have to any divorce, annulment or separation action which may be hereafter brought by the other.

2. The Husband shall have the right to dispose of his property by Last Will and Testament in such manner as he may, in his uncontrolled discretion deem proper, and with the same force and effect as if the Wife had died during his lifetime. The Husband covenants that he will permit any Will of the Wife to be probated, and if she shall die intestate, will allow administration of her personal estate and effects to be taken out by the person or persons who would have been entitled thereto had he died during her lifetime.

3. The Wife shall have the right to dispose of her property by Last Will and Testament in such manner as she may, in her uncontrolled discretion deem proper, and with the same force and effect as if the Husband had died during her lifetime. The Wife covenants that she will permit any Will of the Husband to be probated, and if he shall die intestate, will allow administration of his personal estate and effects to be taken out by the person or persons who would have been entitled thereto had he died during her lifetime.

ARTICLE X—RELEASE AND WAIVER OF MARITAL PROPERTY

Each party does hereby waive and release any statutory right or interest he or she may have by force of law, or otherwise, as a surviving spouse, in the property, real or personal, of which the other party shall die seized or possessed, or to which either of them or their estates may in any way be entitled an each party further waives the right that he or she may now or may hereafter have pursuant to *[the applicable state's estate law]*, or any comparable provisions of the laws of any other state which may have jurisdiction over the estate of either party hereto on his or her death, as such sections or provisions now exist or may hereafter be amended, to elect to take in contravention of the terms of any Last Will and Testament of the other party, including any Last Will and Testament now executed or which may hereafter be executed.

ARTICLE XI—RECONCILIATION

1. This Agreement shall not be invalidated or otherwise affected by reconciliation between the parties hereto, or resumption of marital relations between them, unless said reconciliation or said resumption be documented in a written statement executed and acknowledged by the parties with respect to said reconciliation and/or resumption and, in addition, setting forth that they are canceling this Agreement. This Agreement shall not be invalidated or otherwise affected by an decree or

judgment of separation or divorce made in any court in any action presently pending or which may hereafter be instituted by either party against the other for separation or divorce.

2. Each party agrees that the provisions of this Agreement shall be submitted to any Court in which either may be seeking or may seek a judgment or decree of divorce, annulment, separation or a judgment that otherwise affects their marital status. Each party agrees further that, in the event that a judgment or decree of divorce, annulment, separation, or a judgment or decree which otherwise affects their marital status, is entered, the provisions of this Agreement shall be incorporated into said judgment or decree with such specificity as the Court may deem permissible and by reference as may be appropriate under the law and rules of the Court. However, notwithstanding such incorporation, the obligations and covenants of this Agreement shall survive any decree or judgment of divorce, annulment, or separation or any decree or judgment which otherwise affects their marital status and shall not merge therein, and this Agreement may be enforced independently of said decree or judgment in accordance with the terms hereof.

ARTICLE XII—GENERAL PROVISIONS

1. This Agreement shall be binding upon the parties, the heirs, personal representatives and assigns.

2. This Agreement shall be construed according to the laws of the State of *[Insert Name of State]*, as an agreement made and to be executed within such State.

3. Each party shall take any and all steps and execute and deliver any and all instruments and documents which may be reasonably required for the purpose of giving full force and effect to the provisions of this Agreement.

4. Each party has made independent inquiry into the complete financial circumstances of the other and is fully informed of the income, assets, property and financial prospects of the other.

5. This Agreement constitutes the entire understanding of the parties and no modification or waiver of its terms shall be valid unless in writing and signed by the parties. This Agreement shall not be subject to modification by any court of law. No waiver of a breach or default of any provision of this Agreement shall be deemed a waiver of any subsequent breach or default.

6. In the event that any provision of this Agreement is held to be illegal, invalid, unenforceable, or against public policy, the remaining provisions of the Agreement shall remain valid and enforceable.

7. The Social Security Number of the Husband is *[Insert SS#]*. The Social Security Number of the Wife is *[Insert SS#]*.

8. This Agreement contains the entire understanding of the parties, and there are no representations, warranties, covenants or undertakings other than those expressly set forth herein.

9. This Agreement may be executed simultaneously in counterparts, each of which shall be deemed to be an original.

IN WITNESS WHEREOF, the parties hereto have set their hands and seals the day and year first written above.

_____

Signature Line—Wife

_____

Signature Line—Husband

STATE OF

COUNTY OF

On the _____ day of _____, 2001, before me personally came *[Name of Husband and Name of Wife]*, to me known and known to me to be the individuals described in and who executed the foregoing Agreement, and they acknowledged to me that they executed the same.

Notary Public Stamp and Signature

APPENDIX 12:
DIVORCE STATUTES—LEGAL GROUNDS
FOR DIVORCE

JURISDICTION	LEGAL GROUNDS
Alabama	No-fault; traditional; incompatibility; living separate and apart for 2 years; judicial separation
Alaska	No-fault; traditional; incompatibility; judicial separation
Arizona	No-fault; traditional; judicial separation
Arkansas	No-fault; traditional; living separate and apart for 18 months; judicial separation
California	No-fault; judicial separation
Colorado	No-fault; judicial separation
Connecticut	No-fault; traditional; living separate and apart for 18 months; judicial separation
Delaware	No-fault; living separate and apart for 6 months
District of Columbia	No-fault; Living separate and apart for 1 year; judicial separation
Florida	No-fault
Georgia	No-fault; traditional
Hawaii	No-fault; living separate and apart for 2 years; judicial separation
Idaho	No-fault; traditional; judicial separation
Illinois	No-fault; traditional; living separate and apart for 2 years; judicial separation
Indiana	No-fault; traditional; judicial separation

JURISDICTION	LEGAL GROUNDS
Iowa	No-fault; judicial separation
Kansas	No-fault; traditional; incompatibility; judicial separation
Kentucky	No-fault; living separate and apart for 60 days; judicial separation
Louisiana	No-fault; traditional; living separate and apart for 6 months; judicial separation
Maine	No-fault; traditional; judicial separation
Maryland	No-fault; traditional; living separate and apart for 2 years
Massachusetts	No-fault; traditional; judicial separation
Michigan	No-fault; judicial separation
Minnesota	No-fault; living separate and apart for 60 days; judicial separation
Mississippi	No-fault; traditional
Missouri	No-fault; traditional; living separate and apart for 1 year; judicial separation
Montana	No-fault; incompatibility; living separate and apart for 180 days; judicial separation
Nebraska	No-fault; judicial separation
Nevada	Incompatibility; living separate and apart for 1 year; judicial separation
New Hampshire	No-fault; traditional; living separate and apart for 2 years
New Jersey	No-fault; traditional; living separate and apart for 18 months
New Mexico	No-fault; traditional; incompatibility; judicial separation
New York	Traditional; living separate and apart for 1 year; judicial separation
North Carolina	No-fault; living separate and apart for 1 year; judicial separation
North Dakota	No-fault; traditional; judicial separation
Ohio	No-fault; traditional; incompatibility; living separate and apart for 1 year

JURISDICTION	LEGAL GROUNDS
Oklahoma	Incompatibility; judicial separation
Oregon	No-fault; judicial separation
Pennsylvania	No-fault; traditional; living separate and apart for 2 years
Rhode Island	No-fault; traditional; living separate and apart for 3 years; judicial separation
South Carolina	No-fault; traditionanl; living separate and apart for 1 year; judicial separation
South Dakota	No-fault; traditional; judicial separation
Tennessee	No-fault; traditional; living separate and apart for 2 years; judicial separation
Texas	No-fault; traditional; living separate and apart for 3 years
Utah	No-fault; traditional; living separate and apart for 3 years; judicial separation
Vermont	No-fault; traditional; living separate and apart for 6 months
Virginia	No-fault; traditional; living separate and apart for 1 year; judicial separation
Washington	No-fault
West Virginia	No-fault; traditional; living separate and apart for 1 year; judicial separation
Wisconsin	No-fault; judicial separation
Wyoming	No-fault; traditional; incompatibility; judicial separation[1]

---

1   Source: American Bar Association, Family Law Section.

APPENDIX 13:
DIVORCE STATUTES—RESIDENCY
REQUIREMENTS

Alabama	6 months
Alaska	30 days
Arizona	90 days
Arkansas	60 days
California	6 months
Colorado	90 days
Connecticut	1 year
Delaware	6 months
District of Columbia	6 months
Florida	6 months
Georgia	6 months
Hawaii	6 months
Idaho	6 weeks
Illinois	90 days
Indiana	60 days
Iowa	1 year
Kansas	60 days
Kentucky	180 days
Louisiana	6 months
Maine	6 months

Maryland	None; 1 year
Massachusetts	None
Michigan	6 months
Minnesota	180 days
Mississippi	6 months
Missouri	90 days
Montana	90 days
Nebraska	1 year
Nevada	6 weeks
New Hampshire	1 year
New Jersey	1 year
New Mexico	6 months
New York	1 year;
North Carolina	6 months
North Dakota	6 months
Ohio	6 months
Oklahoma	90 days
Oregon	6 months
Pennsylvania	6 months
Rhode Island	1 year
South Carolina	3 months where both parties are residents
South Dakota	None
Tennessee	6 months
Texas	6 months
Utah	90 days
Vermont	6 months
Virginia	6 months
Washington	1 year
West Virginia	1 year

Wisconsin	6 months
Wyoming	60 days[1]

---

1   Source: American Bar Association, Family Law Section.

APPENDIX 14:
SAMPLE SUMMONS AND VERIFIED COMPLAINT

SUPREME COURT OF THE STATE OF
NEW YORK COUNTY OF _____
————————————————————————X

                Plaintiff,

      -against-

             Defendant.

————————————————————————X

Index No.:_____
Date filed:_____
Plaintiff designates
_____ County
as the place of trial.

The basis of venue is:
_____

SUMMONS WITH NOTICE

Plaintiff/Defendant resides at
_____
_____

ACTION FOR A DIVORCE

To the above named Defendant:

YOU ARE HEREBY SUMMONED to answer the complaint in this action and to serve a copy of your answer on the Plaintiff's Attorney(s) within twenty (20) days after the service of this summons, exclusive of the day of service, where service is made by delivery upon you personally within the state, or within thirty (30) days after completion of service where service is made in any other manner. In case of your failure to appear or answer, judgment will be taken against you by default for the relief demanded in the complaint.

Dated:_____   _____
                         Attorney(s) for Plaintiff
                         Address:
                         Phone No.:

SUPREME COURT OF THE STATE OF   Index No.:
NEW YORK COUNTY OF_____
_____X

Plaintiff

-against-   **VERIFIED COMPLAINT**

                            ACTION FOR DIVORCE

Defendant.

_____-X

FIRST: Plaintiff herein, by his/her attorney, complaining of the Defendant, alleges that the parties are over the age of 18 years and;

SECOND: The Plaintiff has resided in New York State for a continuous period in excess of two years immediately preceding the commencement of this action.

OR

The Defendant has resided in New York State for a continuous period in excess of two years immediately preceding the commencement of this action.

OR

The Plaintiff has resided in New York State for a continuous period in excess of one year immediately preceding the commencement of this action, and:

     a. ____ the parties were married in New York State.

     b. ____ the Plaintiff has lived as husband or wife in New York State with the Defendant.

     c. ____ the cause of action occurred in New York State.

OR

The Defendant has resided in New York State for a continuous period in excess of one year immediately preceding the commencement of this action, and:

     a. ____ the parties were married in New York State.

     b. ____ the Defendant has lived as husband or wife in New York State with the Plaintiff.

     c. ____ the cause of action occurred in New York State.

OR

The cause of action occurred in New York State and both parties were residents thereof at the time of the commencement of this action.

THIRD: The Plaintiff and the Defendant were married on [Insert Date] in [city, town or village; state or country]

The marriage was/was not performed by a clergyman, minister or by a leader of the Society for Ethical Culture.

(If so, check the appropriate box below)

_____ To the best of my knowledge I have taken all steps solely within my power to remove any barrier to the Defendant's remarriage.

OR

_____ I will take prior to the entry of final judgment all steps solely within my power to the best of my knowledge to remove any barrier to the Defendant's remarriage.

OR

_____ The Defendant has waived in writing the requirements of DRL §253 (Barriers Remarriage).

FOURTH: There are no children of the marriage.

OR

There is (are) _____ child(ren) of the marriage, namely:

Name	Date of Birth	Address
_____	_____	
_____	_____	
_____	_____	_____
_____		

The Plaintiff resides at _____

The Defendant resides at_____

The parties are covered by the following group health plans:

Plaintiff	**Defendant**
Group Health Plan:_____	Group Health Plan:_____
Address:_____	Address:_____
Identification Number:_____	Identification Number:_____

Plan Administrator:_____   Plan Administrator:_____

Type of Coverage:_____   Type of Coverage:_____

FIFTH: The grounds for divorce that are alleged as follows:

[Strike Inapplicable Grounds]

Cruel and Inhuman Treatment (DRL §170(1)):

At the following times, none of which are earlier than (5) years prior to commencement of this action, the Defendant engaged in conduct that so endangered the mental and physical well-being of the Plaintiff, so as to render it unsafe and improper for the parties to cohabit (live together) as husband and wife.

(State the facts that demonstrate cruel and inhuman conduct giving dates, places and specific acts. Conduct may include physical, verbal, sexual or emotional behavior.)

Abandonment (DRL 170(2):

That commencing on or about _____, and continuing for a period of more than one (1) year immediately prior to commencement of this action, the Defendant left the marital residence of the parties located at [Insert address] and did not return. Such absence was without cause or justification, and was without Plaintiff's consent.

That commencing on or about _____, and continuing for a period of more than one (1) year immediately prior to commencement of this action, the Defendant refused to have sexual relations with the Plaintiff despite Plaintiff's repeated requests to resume such relations. Defendant does not suffer from any disability which would prevent her/him from engaging in such sexual relations with Plaintiff. The refusal to engage in sexual relations was without good cause or justification and occurred at the marital residence located at [Insert address].

That commencing on or about _____, and continuing for a period of more than one (1) year immediately prior to commencement of this action, the Defendant willfully and without cause or justification abandoned the Plaintiff, who had been a faithful and dutiful husband/wife, by depriving Plaintiff of access to the marital residence located at [Insert address]   This deprivation of access was without the consent of the Plaintiff and continued for a period of greater than one year.

Confinement to Prison (DRL §170(3)):

(a) That after the marriage of Plaintiff and Defendant, Defendant was confined in prison for a period of three or more consecutive years, to wit: that Defendant was confined in _____ prison on _____, and has remained confined to this date; and

(b) not more that five (5) years has elapsed between the end of the third year of imprisonment and the date of commencement of this action.

Adultery (DRL §170(4)):

(a) That on _____, at the premises located at [Insert address], the Defendant engaged in sexual intercourse with _____, without the procurement nor the connivance of the Plaintiff, and the Plaintiff ceased to cohabit (live) with the Defendant upon the discovery of the adultery; and

(b) not more than five (5) years elapsed between the date of said adultery and the date of commencement of this action.

(Attach a corroborating affidavit of a third party witness or other additional proof).

Living Separate and Apart Pursuant to a Separation Decree or Judgment of Separation (DRL §170(5)):

(a) That the _____ Court, _____ County, _____ (Country or State) rendered a decree or judgment of separation on _____, under Index Number _____; and

(b) that the parties have lived separate and apart for a period of one year or longer after the granting of such decree; and

(c) that the Plaintiff has substantially complied with all the terms and conditions of such decree or judgment.

Living Separate and Apart Pursuant to a Separation Agreement (DRL §170(6)):

(a) That the Plaintiff and Defendant entered into a written agreement of separation, which they subscribed and acknowledged on _____, in the form required to entitle a deed to be recorded; and

(b) that the agreement/memorandum of said agreement was filed on_____ in the Office of the Clerk of the County of _____, wherein Plaintiff/Defendant resided; and

(c) that the parties have lived separate and apart for a period of one year or longer after the execution of said agreement; and

(d) that the Plaintiff has substantially complied with all terms and conditions of such agreement.

SIXTH: There is no judgment in any court for a divorce and no other matrimonial action between the parties pending in this court or in any other court of competent jurisdiction.

WHEREFORE, Plaintiff demands judgment against the Defendant as follows: A judgment dissolving the marriage between the parties

AND

equitable distribution of marital property;

OR

marital property to be distributed pursuant to the annexed separation agreement / stipulation;

OR

I waive equitable distribution of marital property;

AND

and any other relief the court deems fitting and proper.

Dated:

_____   _____
                         Attorney(s) for Plaintiff
                         Address:
                         Phone No.:

VERIFICATION

STATE OF NEW YORK

COUNTY OF

I _____ (Print Name), am the Plaintiff in the within action for a divorce. I have read the foregoing complaint and know the contents thereof. The contents are true to my own knowledge except as to matters therein stated to be alleged upon information and belief, and as to those matters I believe them to be true.

_____

Plaintiff's Signature

Subscribed and Sworn to
before me on [Date].

_____

NOTARY PUBLIC

Source: New York State Unified Court System.

APPENDIX 15:
SAMPLE POOR PERSON ORDER

PRESENT:

HON._____
  Justice of the Supreme Court

_____X

In the Matter of the Application of   Index No.:_____

_____,   Plaintiff,

For Permission to Prosecute an
Action as a Poor Person   **POOR PERSON ORDER**

       -against-

_____,   Defendant.

_____X

Upon the annexed affidavit of_____, Plaintiff, And it being alleged that said Plaintiff has a good cause of action or claim that *he/she* is unable to pay the costs, fees and expenses to prosecute this action, and that there is no other person beneficially interested in the action, thereof

NOW on motion of Plaintiff, it is hereby

ORDERED that Plaintiff is permitted to prosecute this action as a poor person against_____ , Defendant, and it is further

ORDERED that any recovery by Judgment or Settlement in favor of Plaintiff shall be paid to the Clerk of the Court to await distribution pursuant to court order, and it is further

ORDERED that the Clerk of this Court is directed to make no charge for costs or fees in connection with the prosecution of this action, including one (1) certified copy of the judgment.

E N T E R:

_____

Justice of the Supreme Court

Source: New York State Unified Court System.

APPENDIX 16:
CERTIFICATE OF DISSOLUTION OF MARRIAGE

LOCAL INDEX NUMBER

STATE FILE NUMBER

New York State
Department of Health
CERTIFICATE OF DISSOLUTION OF MARRIAGE

TYPE, OR PRINT IN PERMANENT BLACK INK

HUSBAND

1. HUSBAND – NAME: FIRST MIDDLE LAST	1 A. SOCIAL SECURITY NUMBER

| 2. DATE OF BIRTH Month Day Year | 3. STATE OF BIRTH (COUNTRY IF NOT USA) | 4.A RESIDENCE: STATE | 4B. COUNTY | 4C. LOCALITY (CHECK ONE AND SPECIFY) ☐ CITY OF ☐ TOWN OF ☐ VILLAGE OF |

| 4D. STREET AND NUMBER OF RESIDENCE (INCLUDE ZIP CODE) | 4E. IF CITY OR VILLAGE, IS RESIDENCE WITHIN CITY OR VILLAGE LIMITS? YES ☐ NO ☐ IF NO, SPECIFY TOWN: |

| 5A. ATTORNEY - NAME | 5B. ADDRESS (INCLUDE ZIP CODE) |

WIFE

| 6A. WIFE - NAME FIRST MIDDLE LAST | 6B. MAIDEN | 6C. SOCIAL SECURITY NUMBER |

| 7. DATE OF BIRTH Month Day Year | 8. STATE OF BIRTH (COUNTRY IF NOT USA) | 9.A RESIDENCE: STATE | 9B. COUNTY | 9C. LOCALITY (CHECK ONE AND SPECIFY) ☐ CITY OF ☐ TOWN OF ☐ VILLAGE OF |

| 9D. STREET AND NUMBER OF RESIDENCE (INCLUDE ZIP CODE) | 9E. IF CITY OR VILLAGE, IS RESIDENCE WITHIN CITY OR VILLAGE LIMITS? YES ☐ NO ☐ IF NO, SPECIFY TOWN: |

| 10A. ATTORNEY - NAME | 10B. ADDRESS (INCLUDE ZIP CODE) |

| 11A. PLACE OF THIS MARRIAGE - CITY, TOWN OR VILLAGE | 11B. COUNTY | 11C. STATE (COUNTRY IF NOT USA) |

| 12A. DATE OF THIS MARRIAGE Month Day Year | 12B. APPROXIMATE DATE COUPLE SEPARATED Month Year | 13A. NUMBER OF CHILDREN EVER BORN ALIVE OF THIS MARRIAGE (SPECIFY) | 13B. NUMBER OF CHILDREN UNDER 18 IN THIS FAMILY (SPECIFY) |

DECREE

| 14A. I CERTIFY THAT A DECREE OF DISSOLUTION OF THE ABOVE MARRIAGE WAS RENDERED ON Month Day Year | 14B. DATE OF ENTRY: Month Day Year | 14C. TYPE OF DECREE - DIVORCE, ANNULMENT, OTHER DISSOLUTION (SPECIFY) |

| 14D. COUNTY OF DECREE | 14E. TITLE OF COURT |

14F. SIGNATURE OF COUNTY CLERK
>

CONFIDENTIAL INFORMATION

HUSBAND

15. RACE: WHITE, BLACK, AMERICAN INDIAN, OTHER (SPECIFY)	16. NUMBER OF THIS MARRIAGE - FIRST, SECOND, ETC. (SPECIFY)	17. IF PREVIOUSLY MARRIED HOW MANY ENDED BY		18. EDUCATION: INDICATE HIGHEST GRADE COMPLETED ONLY
		A. DEATH NUMBER____ NONE ☐	B. DIVORCE OR ANNULMENT NUMBER____ NONE ☐	ELEMENTARY 0 1 2 3 4 5 6 7 8 / HIGH SCHOOL 1 2 3 4 / COLLEGE 1 2 3 4 5+

WIFE

19. RACE: WHITE, BLACK, AMERICAN INDIAN, OTHER (SPECIFY)	20. NUMBER OF THIS MARRIAGE - FIRST, SECOND, ETC. (SPECIFY)	21. IF PREVIOUSLY MARRIED HOW MANY ENDED BY		22. EDUCATION: INDICATE HIGHEST GRADE COMPLETED ONLY
		A. DEATH NUMBER____ NONE ☐	B. DIVORCE OR ANNULMENT NUMBER____ NONE ☐	ELEMENTARY 0 1 2 3 4 5 6 7 8 / HIGH SCHOOL 1 2 3 4 / COLLEGE 1 2 3 4 5+

| 23. PLAINTIFF - HUSBAND, WIFE, OTHER (SPECIFY) | 24. DECREE GRANTED TO HUSBAND, WIFE, OTHER (SPECIFY) | 25. LEGAL GROUNDS FOR DECREE (SPECIFY) |

| 26. SIGNATURE OF PERSON PREPARING CERTIFICATE > | ATTORNEY AT LAW |

NOTE: Social Security Numbers of the husband and wife are mandatory. They are required by New York State Public Health Law Section 4139 and 42 U.S.C. 666(a). They may be used for child support enforcement purposes.

DOH-2168 (5/2000)

APPENDIX 17:
DIVORCE STATUTES—PROPERTY
DIVISION

JURISDICTION	TYPE OF PROPERTY DIVISION
Alabama	Equitable Distribution of Marital Property
Alaska	Equitable Distribution of Marital Property
Arizona	Community Property
Arkansas	Equitable Distribution of Marital Property
California	Community Property
Colorado	Equitable Distribution of Marital Property
Connecticut	Equitable Distribution of Marital Property
Delaware	Equitable Distribution of Marital Property
District of Columbia	Equitable Distribution of Marital Property
Florida	Equitable Distribution of Marital Property
Georgia	Equitable Distribution of Marital Property
Hawaii	Equitable Distribution of Marital Property
Idaho	Community Property
Illinois	Equitable Distribution of Marital Property
Indiana	Equitable Distribution of Marital Property
Iowa	Equitable Distribution of Marital Property
Kansas	Equitable Distribution of Marital Property
Kentucky	Equitable Distribution of Marital Property
Louisiana	Community Property

JURISDICTION	TYPE OF PROPERTY DIVISION
Maine	Equitable Distribution of Marital Property
Maryland	Equitable Distribution of Marital Property
Massachusetts	Equitable Distribution of Marital Property
Michigan	Equitable Distribution of Marital Property
Minnesota	Equitable Distribution of Marital Property
Mississippi	Equitable Distribution of Marital Property
Missouri	Equitable Distribution of Marital Property
Montana	Equitable Distribution of Marital Property
Nebraska	Equitable Distribution of Marital Property
Nevada	Community Property
New Hampshire	Equitable Distribution of Marital Property
New Jersey	Equitable Distribution of Marital Property
New Mexico	Community Property
New York	Equitable Distribution of Marital Property
North Carolina	Equitable Distribution of Marital Property
North Dakota	Equitable Distribution of Marital Property
Ohio	Equitable Distribution of Marital Property
Oklahoma	Equitable Distribution of Marital Property
Oregon	Equitable Distribution of Marital Property
Pennsylvania	Equitable Distribution of Marital Property
Rhode Island	Equitable Distribution of Marital Property
South Carolina	Equitable Distribution of Marital Property
South Dakota	Equitable Distribution of Marital Property
Tennessee	Equitable Distribution of Marital Property
Texas	Community Property
Utah	Equitable Distribution of Marital Property
Vermont	Equitable Distribution of Marital Property
Virginia	Equitable Distribution of Marital Property
Washington	Community Property

JURISDICTION	TYPE OF PROPERTY DIVISION
West Virginia	Equitable Distribution of Marital Property
Wisconsin	Community Property
Wyoming	Equitable Distribution of Marital Property[1]

---

1   Source: American Bar Association, Family Law Section.

APPENDIX 18:
FINANCIAL DISCLOSURE AFFIDAVIT

F.C.A. §413-1, 424-a; Art. 5-B
D.R.L. §236-B, 240

Form 4-17
(Financial Disclosure
Affidavit)
9/99

FAMILY COURT OF THE STATE OF NEW YORK
COUNTY OF
....
In the Matter of a Proceeding for Support

Docket No.

(Commissioner of Social Services, Assignor,
on behalf of   , Assignee)

                                                                FINANCIAL
                      Petitioner   DISCLOSURE
S.S.# (Assignor)   AFFIDAVIT

          -against-

                      Respondent.
S.S.#
....

NOTICE: YOU ARE REQUIRED TO ATTACH TO THIS FORM A CURRENT AND
REPRESENTATIVE PAYCHECK STUB AND A COPY OF YOUR MOST RECENTLY FILED STATE
AND FEDERAL INCOME TAX RETURNS, INCLUDING A COPY OF THE W-2 WAGE AND TAX
STATEMENT(S) SUBMITTED WITH THE RETURNS. YOU MAY ALSO BE REQUIRED TO
PRODUCE OTHER PAYCHECK STUBS, EMPLOYMENT OR BUSINESS RECORDS AND PROOF OF
CLAIMED EXPENSES. IN ADDITION, YOU ARE REQUIRED TO PROVIDE INFORMATION
RELATING TO ALL GROUP HEALTH PLANS AVAILABLE TO YOU FOR THE PROVISION OF
CARE OR OTHER MEDICAL BENEFITS FOR THE CHILD(REN) FOR WHOM SUPPORT IS
SOUGHT.

STATE OF NEW YORK   )
                         ):ss.:
COUNTY OF   )

_____ , the (Petitioner) (Respondent) herein, residing at _____
_____ , being duly sworn, deposes and says that the following is an accurate
statement of my income from all sources, my liabilities, my assets and my net worth, from whatever
sources, and whatever kind and nature, and wherever situated:

I. INCOME FROM ALL SOURCES: The correct amount of the child support obligation is presumed to
be a percentage of income as defined by law. The percentages are set forth in Addendum A. Other pertinent
information is set forth in Addenda B and C. List your income from all sources as follows:

---

a. <u>Wages and Salaries</u> (as reportable on Federal and State income tax returns):

     1 . Employer and address_____
     2 . Number of members in household_____
     3. Number of dependents _____
     4. Hours worked per week_____
     5. Weekly gross salary/wages _____
     6. Weekly deductions:_____
        a. Social Security (FICA) Tax _____
        b. New York State Tax _____
        c. Federal Tax _____
        d. Other payroll deductions_____
     7. Income of other members of household _____

NOTE: ATTACH INFORMATION FOR ADDITIONAL EMPLOYERS SEPARATELY TO THIS FORM.

b. <u>Self-Employment Income</u> (Describe and list self- employment income; attach to this form the most recently filed Federal and State income tax returns, including all schedules):_____
_____
_____
_____
_____

c. <u>Interest/Dividend Income:</u> _____
_____

d. <u>Other Income:</u>
     1. Workers Compensation _____
     2. Disability Benefits _____
     3. Unemployment Insurance Benefits _____
     4. Social Security Benefits _____
     5. Veterans Benefits _____
     6. Pensions and Retirement Benefits _____
     7. Fellowships/Stipends/Annuities _____

e. <u>Income from other sources:</u> (List here and explain any other income including but not limited to: non-income producing assets; employment 'perks' and reimbursed expenses; fringe benefits as a result of employment; periodic income, personal injury settlements; non-reported income; and money, goods and services provided by relatives and friends)_____
_____
_____

II. ASSETS: The Court can consider the assets of the custodial parent and/or the non-custodial parent in its award of child support. List your assets as follows:

a. Savings account balance (Name of bank: _____)   a)$_____

Form 4-17 page 3

b. Checking account balance (Name of bank: _____)   b) $_____

c. Automobile(s) (Year and make: _____)   c) $_____

   Loan information _____

d. Residence owned (Address: _____)   d) $_____

e. Other real estate owned _____   e) $_____

f. Other assets (For example: stocks, bonds, trailers, boat, etc.) _____   f) $_____

g. Driver's, professional, recreational, sporting and other licenses and permits held (provide name of issuing agency, license number and attach a copy if possible)_____

_____

NOTE: ATTACH TO THIS FORM ANY INFORMATION AS TO ANY ADDITIONAL ASSETS.

III .DEDUCTIONS FROM INCOME: The Court allows certain deductions from income prior to applying the child support percentages. List the deductions that apply to you as follows:

a. Unreimbursed employee business expenses   a) $_____

b. Maintenance actually paid to spouse not a party to this action*   b) $_____

c. Maintenance actually paid to spouse who is a party to this action   c) $_____

d. Child support actually paid on behalf of non- subject child(ren)*   d) $_____

e. Family Assistance   e) $_____

f. Supplemental Security Income   f) $_____

g. NYC/Yonkers Income Tax   g) $_____

h. FICA   h) $_____

     *Attach to this form a copy of the appropriate Court Order

IV. HEALTH INSURANCE, UNREIMBURSED HEALTH-RELATED EXPENSES, CHILD CARE EXPENSES AND EDUCATIONAL EXPENSES: As part of the child support obligation, parents shall be directed to provide health insurance, pay a pro-rated share of unreimbursed health- related expenses, pay a pro-rated share of child care expenses and in the Court's discretion pay educational expenses. List your information as follows and cross out or delete inapplicable provisions:

a. I (have) (do not have) health insurance coverage (through employment) (privately purchased) (through the "Child Health Plus" program).

   1. My coverage includes (dental) (prescription drug) (optical) (other health care services or benefits [specify]:   ).

   2. The portion of the cost of the insurance paid by my employer or through my employment is $ The cost of the insurance paid by me is $ _____ .

   3. The person(s) covered by my insurance is/are:_____

   _____

   4. My policy number is _____ .

   5. Coverage (does)(does not) presently include my child(ren). The additional cost to me to include my child(ren) would be [specify cost for each type of benefit; if benefit

unavailable,

   so indicate]:

     Medical: $_____ per _____. Optical: $_____ per _____.

     Dental: $_____ per _____. Prescription drugs: $_____ per _____.

Other Health Services or Benefits [specify]:_____ $_____ per _____.

6. The name and address of my primary (and secondary) health insurer is/are: _____
_____

7. My primary (and secondary) health plan administrator is/are: (indicate name, address and telephone number of contact person for employer or organization):_____
_____

8. There are (medical) (dental) (prescription drug) (optical) (other health care benefits [specify]:
_____) insurance benefits available to the child(ren) through
an individual who is not a party to this action. This individual is [indicate name and relationship]: ____
_____ . These benefits cost as follows:
_____ .

b. My child care provider is: _____. The average
number of hours of child care incurred per week are: _____

c. My child's educational needs and expenses are: _____
_____

V. VARIANCE FROM THE PERCENTAGES: The Family Court Act allows the Court to order support different from the percentages if the Court finds that the support based upon the percentages would be unjust or inappropriate due to certain factors. <u>The factors are set forth in Addendum D.</u> The following is/are the factor(s) that the Court should consider in this case: _____
_____

VI. EXPENSES: In ordering support by the percentages the Court is not obligated to consider expenses. However, if the Court varies from the percentages, expenses may be considered. List your expenses as follows: [List all expenses on a weekly or monthly basis; however, you must be consistent: if any items are paid monthly, divide by 4 to obtain the weekly payment; if any items are paid weekly, multiply by 4 to obtain the monthly payment).
(Please specify)]: I am listing my expenses on a (weekly)(monthly) basis:

a. Rent or mortgage payment   a) $ _____
b. Mortgage interest and amortization   b) $ _____
c. Realty taxes (if not included in mortgage payment)   c) $ _____
d. Insurance on realty   d) $_____
e. Utilities: gas_____ electric/ water_____ telephone _____ cable _____   e) $ _____
f. Garbage collection   f) $_____
g. Household repairs (specify:_____   g) $_____
h. Food   h) $_____
i. Charge accounts, loans, etc. 1)_____   i) $ _____
(from Section VII below)   2)_____
       3)_____

j. Automobile expenses: gas _____ maintenance _____ insurance & fees _____

Form 4-17 page 5

loan_____   j)$ _____
k. Public transportation   k)$_____
l. Life insurance   l)$_____
m.Health insurance   m)$ _____
n. Clothing : self $_____others $ _____ (explain:_____) n)$ _____
o. Laundry and dry cleaning   o)$ _____
p. Education and tuition (explain:_____) p)$ _____
q. Child care   q)$_____
r. Contributions   r)$ _____
s. Union dues (mandatory: yes_____ no _____)   s)$_____
t. Entertainment   t)$_____
u. Miscellaneous personal expenses (specify:_____) u)$ _____
v. Other (specify:_____) v)$ _____

VII. LIABILITIES, LOANS AND DEBTS: In ordering support by the percentages the Court is not obligated to consider liabilities, loans, and debts. However, if the Court varies from the percentages, they may be considered. List your liabilities, loans and debts as follows:

Creditor _____ Creditor _____   Creditor _____
    Purpose_____   Purpose_____   Purpose_____
    Date incurred_____   Date incurred_____   Date incurred_____
    Total balance due_____   Total balance due_____   Total balance due_____

NOTE: ATTACH TO THIS FORM INFORMATION REGARDING ANY ADDITIONAL DEBTS.

VIII: LIFE AND ACCIDENT INSURANCE: The Court may direct you to purchase and maintain life and/or accident insurance benefits or assign benefits on existing policies for the benefit of your children. List your insurance policy or policies as follows:

a. Life insurance: (Name of insurer):_____ $_____
    (Beneficiary/Beneficiaries):_____

    (Name of insurer):_____ $_____
    (Beneficiary/Beneficiaries):_____

b. Accident insurance: (Name of insurer):_____ $_____
    (Name of insurer):_____ $_____

Form 4-17 page 6

This information is current as of (specify date)_____ .

_____
(Petitioner)(Respondent)

_____
Print or Type Name

_____
Signature of Attorney, if any

_____
Attorney's Name (Print or Type)

_____
_____
_____
Attorney's Address and Telephone Number

I have carefully read the foregoing statement and attest to its truth and accuracy.
Sworn to before me this_____
day of_____ , _____ .

_____
(Deputy)Clerk of the Court
    Notary Public

ADDENDUM A
CHILD SUPPORT PERCENTAGES

The child support percentages that shall be applied by the Court unless the Court makes a finding that the non-custodial parent's share is unjust or inappropriate are as follows: 17% for one child; 25% for two children; 29% for three children; 31% for five children; and no less than 35% for five or more children.

ADDENDUM B
COMBINED PARENTAL INCOME OVER $80,000.00

Where combined parental income exceeds $80,000.00, the Court shall determine the amount of child support for the amount of the combined parental income in excess of such dollar amount through consideration of the factors set forth in Addendum D and or the support percentage set forth in Addendum A.

ADDENDUM C

Form 4-17 page 7

SELF-SUPPORT RESERVE

Where the annual amount of the basic child support obligation would reduce the non -custodial parent's income below the poverty income guidelines amount for a single person as reported by the federal Department of Health and Human Services , the basic child support obligation shall be twenty-five dollars per month unless the interests of justice dictate otherwise. Where the annual amount of the basic child support obligation would reduce the non-custodial parent's income below the self-support reserve but not below, the proverty income guidelines amount of a single person as reported by the federal Department of Health and Human Services, the basic child support obligation shall be fifty dollars per month or the difference between the non-custodial parent's income and the self-support reserve, whichever is greater.

ADDENDUM D
VARIANCE FROM THE PERCENTAGES

The Court has the discretion to vary from the percentages if it finds that the non-custodial parent's pro-rata share of the basic child support obligation is unjust or inappropriate. This finding shall be based upon consideration of the following factors:

1 . The financial resources of the custodial and non-custodial parent, and those of the child.

2.The physical and emotional health of the child and his/her special needs and aptitudes.

3.The standard of living the child would have enjoyed had the marriage or household not been dissolved.

4.The tax consequences to the parties.

5.The non-monetary contributions that the parents will make toward the care and well-being of the child.

6.The educational needs of either parent.

7.A determination that the gross income of one parent is substantially less than the other parent's gross income.

8.The needs of the children of the non-custodial parent for whom the non-custodial parent is providing support who are not subject

to the instant action and whose support has not been deducted from income, and the financial resources of any person obligated to support such children, provided, however, that this factor may apply only if the resources available to support such children are less than the resources available to support the children who are subject to the instant action.

9. Provided that the child is not on public assistance (I) extraordinary expenses incurred by the non-custodial parent in exercising visitation, or (ii) expenses incurred by the non-custodial parent in extended visitation provided that the custodial parent's expenses are substantially reduced as a result thereof.

10. Any other factors the Court determines are relevant in each case.

NOTE: The language in the above Addenda is paraphrased from that in the statute for the purposes of simplification. For statutory language, see Family Court Act Sections 413(1) and 424-a and Domestic Relations Law Sections 236-B and 240.

APPENDIX 19:
SAMPLE QUALIFIED DOMESTIC
RELATIONS ORDER

PRESENT: Hon. _____
                    Judge/ Hearing Examiner

_____

In the Matter of a Proceeding for Support
Pursuant to Article ____ of the Family
Court
Act   **QUALIFIED DOMESTIC**
                    Petitioner,   **RELATIONS ORDER**

   - against -

                                         Docket No. _____

                    Respondent.

_____

**THIS ORDER IS INTENDED TO CONSTITUTE A QUALIFIED DOMES-
TIC RELATIONS ORDER WITHIN THE MEANING OF SECTIONS
414(P) AND 401(A)(13) OF THE INTERNAL REVENUE CODE OF
1986 AND SHALL BE ADMINISTERED IN CONFORMITY WITH SUCH
PROVISIONS.**

An order of support having been entered by the Family Court, County of
_____, State of _____, whereby (Respondent) (Petitioner)
was directed to pay the sum of $____ per _____ for the support of
[specify name(s) of spouse and/or name and social security number(s)
of children] to (Petitioner) (Respondent) (and a further sum of
$_____ to be applied to the reduction of arrears until the
amount of $_____ in arrears is paid in full (if applicable));

And the Court having found that [specify name of the "Participant"] has a vested right to a portion of said benefits;

Therefore, it is hereby:

ORDERED that,

1. A portion of the interest of the Participant in the [specify name of

Plan] (herein after referred to as the "Plan")shall be assigned to the Alternate Payee, as specified in this Order.

2. Participant information: The name, last-known address, social security number and date of birth of the plan "Participant" are:

Name:

Address:

Social Security No.:

Date of Birth:

The participant shall have the duty to notify the plan administrator in writing of any changes in his/her mailing address subsequent to the entry of this Order.

3. Alternate Payee Information: The name, last-known address, social security number, and date of birth of the "Alternate Payee" are:

Name:

Address:

Social Security No.:

Date of Birth:

The alternate payee shall have the duty to notify the plan administrator in writing of any changes in his/her mailing address subsequent to the entry of this Order.

4. Of the pension amounts otherwise paid to the Participant during his or her lifetime, $_____ of each payment or, if such amount exceeds the amount of the payment to the Participant, the full amount of the Participant's payment, shall be paid to the Alternate Payee. These payments are to begin with the first payment made to the participant after the order is submitted to the plan.

[Delete following paragraph if inapplicable]:
4a. Of the pension amounts otherwise paid to the Participant during his or her lifetime, an additional $_____of each payment shall be paid instead to the Alternate Payee until the arrears of $_____ are paid in full. If such amount exceeds the amount

of the payment to the Participant, the full amount of the Participant's payment, shall be paid to the Alternate Payee. These payments are to begin with the first payment made to the Participant after the order is submitted to the plan.)

5. No benefit shall be payable under this order if either the Alternate Payee or the Participant dies before commencement of pension benefits under the Plan.

6. Nothing contained in this order shall be construed to require any plan, or plan administrator to:

A) provide to the alternate payee any type, or amount of benefit, or option not otherwise available to the participant under the plan, or

B) to provide the alternate payee increased benefits not available to the participant, or

C) pay any benefits to the alternate payee which are required to be paid to another alternate payee under another order submitted to the plan prior to this order; and it is further

ORDERED, that copies of this order shall be served by (Petitioner) (Petitioner's Attorney) [specify address] to the plan administrator who shall:

a) promptly notify counsel, if any, the participant and the payee of the receipt of a copy of this Order; and

b) within a reasonable period of time after receipt of this order, determine whether the order is acceptable, and notify counsel, if any, the participant and the alternate pay of such determination;

and it is further

ORDERED, that this Order is deemed appropriate to effectuate the division of the retirement benefits earned by, "the participant", as a result of (his)(her) participation in the above noted pension plan; and it is further

ORDERED, that this Court retain jurisdiction to implement and supervise the payment of retirement benefits as provided herein should either party or the plan administrator make such application, and the Court determine that it is appropriate and necessary.

DATED:

_____
JUDGE/HEARING EXAMINER

_____

Source: New York State Unified Court System.

APPENDIX 20:
DIVORCE STATUTES—SPOUSAL SUPPORT FACTORS

JURISDICTION	FACTORS CONSIDERED
Alabama	Standard of living; marital fault relevant
Alaska	Statutory list; standard of living; marital fault not considered
Arizona	Statutory list; standard of living; status as custodial parent; marital fault not considered
Arkansas	Marital fault not considered
California	Statutory list; standard of living; marital fault not considered
Colorado	Statutory list; standard of living; status as custodial parent; marital fault not considered
Connecticut	Statutory list; standard of living; status as custodial parent; marital fault relevant
Delaware	Statutory list; standard of living; status as custodial parent; marital fault not considered
District of Columbia	Standard of living; marital fault relevant
Florida	Statutory list; standard of living; marital fault relevant
Georgia	Statutory list; standard of living; marital fault relevant
Hawaii	Statutory list; standard of living; status as custodial parent; marital fault not considered
Idaho	Statutory list; marital fault relevant

Illinois	Statutory list; standard of living; status as custodial parent; marital fault not considered
Indiana	Statutory list; standard of living; status as custodial parent; marital fault not considered
Iowa	Statutory list; standard of living; status as custodial parent; marital fault not considered
Kansas	Marital fault not considered
Kentucky	Statutory list; standard of living; marital fault relevant
Louisiana	Statutory list; status as custodial parent; marital fault relevant
Maine	Statutory list; marital fault not considered
Maryland	Statutory list; standard of living; marital fault relevant
Massachusetts	Statutory list; standard of living; marital fault relevant
Michigan	Standard of living; marital fault relevant
Minnesota	Statutory list; standard of living; status as custodial parent; marital fault not considered
Mississippi	Marital fault relevant
Missouri	Statutory list; standard of living; status as custodial parent; marital fault relevant
Montana	Statutory list; standard of living; status as custodial parent; marital fault not considered
Nebraska	Statutory list; standard of living; status as custodial parent; marital fault not considered
Nevada	Standard of living; status as custodial parent; marital fault relevant
New Hampshire	Statutory list; standard of living; status as custodial parent; marital fault relevant
New Jersey	Marital Property
New Mexico	Statutory list; standard of living; marital fault not considered
New York	Statutory list; standard of living; status as custodial parent; marital fault relevant
North Carolina	Statutory list; standard of living; marital fault relevant

North Dakota	Standard of living; marital fault relevant
Ohio	Statutory list; marital fault not considered
Oklahoma	Standard of living; status as custodial parent; marital fault not considered
Oregon	Statutory list; standard of living; status as custodial parent; marital fault not considered
Pennsylvania	Statutory list; standard of living; marital fault relevant
Rhode Island	Statutory list; standard of living; status as custodial parent; marital fault relevant
South Carolina	Statutory list; standard of living; status as custodial parent; marital fault relevant
South Dakota	Standard of living; marital fault relevant
Tennessee	Statutory list; standard of living; status as custodial parent; marital fault relevant
Texas	Statutory list; standard of living; status as custodial parent; marital fault relevant
Utah	Statutory list; standard of living; marital fault relevant
Vermont	Statutory list; standard of living; status as custodial parent; marital fault not considered
Virginia	Statutory list; standard of living; marital fault relevant
Washington	Statutory list; standard of living; marital fault not considered
West Virginia	Statutory list; status as custodial parent; marital fault relevant
Wisconsin	Statutory list; standard of living; status as custodial parent; marital fault not considered
Wyoming	Marital fault relevant[1]

---

1   Source: American Bar Association, Family Law Section.

APPENDIX 21:
CHILD SUPPORT WORKSHEET

Note: All numbers used in this worksheet are YEARLY figures. Convert weekly or monthly figures to annualized numbers.

STEP 1

MANDATORY PARENTAL INCOME	FATHER	MOTHER
1. Gross (total) income (as reported on most recent Federal tax return, or as computed in accordance with Internal Revenue Code and regulations)	_____	_____
The following items MUST be added if not already included in Line 1:	_____	_____
2. Investment income:	_____	_____
3. Workers' compensation:	_____	_____
4. Disability benefits:	_____	_____
5. Unemployment insurance benefits:	_____	_____
6. Social Security benefits:	_____	_____
7. Veterans benefits:	_____	_____
8. Pension/retirement income:	_____	_____
9. Fellowships and stipends:	_____	_____
10. Annuity payments:	_____	_____
11. If self-employed, depreciation greater than straight-line depreciation used in determining business income or investment credit:	_____	_____
12. If self-employed, entertainment and travel allowances deducted from business income to the extent the allowances reduce personal expenditures:	_____	_____

STEP 1
MANDATORY PARENTAL INCOME   FATHER   MOTHER

13. Former income voluntarily reduced to avoid child support: _____   _____

14. Income voluntarily deferred: _____   _____

A. TOTAL MANDATORY INCOME: _____   _____

STEP 2
NON-MANDATORY PARENTAL INCOME

These items must be disclosed here. Their inclusion in the final calculations, however, is discretionary. In contested cases, the Court determines whether or not they are included. In uncontested cases, the parents and their attorneys or mediators must determine which should be included.

15. Income attributable to non-income producing assets: _____   _____

16. Employment benefits that confer personal economic benefits: (Such as meals, lodging, memberships, automobiles, other)   _____   _____

_____   _____   _____

_____   _____   _____

_____   _____   _____

17. Fringe benefits of employment: _____   _____

18. Money, goods and services provided by relatives and friends: _____   _____

_____   _____   _____

_____   _____   _____

B. TOTAL NON-MANDATORY INCOME: _____   _____

C. TOTAL INCOME *(add Line A + Line B):*   _____   _____

STEP 3
DEDUCTIONS   _____   _____

19. Expenses of investment income listed on line 2:   _____   _____

20. Unreimbursed business expenses that do not reduce personal expenditures: _____   _____

21. Alimony or maintenance actually paid to a former spouse: _____   _____

STEP 3
DEDUCTIONS

22. Alimony or maintenance paid to the other parent but only if child support will increase when alimony stops:

23. Child support actually paid to other children the parent is legally obligated to support:

24. Public assistance:

25. Supplemental security income:

26. New York City or Yonkers income or earnings taxes actually paid:

27. Social Security taxes (FICA) actually paid:

D. TOTAL DEDUCTIONS:

E. FATHER'S INCOME (Line C minus Line D): $

F. MOTHER'S INCOME (Line C minus Line D): $

STEP 4
G. COMBINED PARENTAL INCOME (Line E + F) $

STEP 5
MULTIPLY Line G (up to $80,000) by the proper percentage (insert in Line H):

For 1 child........................17%   For 3 children.................29%

For 2 children...................25%   For 4 children.................31%

For 5 or more children..............35% (minimum)

H. COMBINED CHILD SUPPORT: $

STEP 6
DIVIDE the noncustodial parent's
amount on Line E or Line F: $

by the amount of Line G: $
to obtain the percentage allocated

I. to the noncustodial parent: _____%

STEP 7
J. MULTIPLY line H by Line I: $

STEP 8

K. DECIDE the amount of child support $_____
to be paid on any combined parental
income exceeding $80,000 per year
using the percentages in STEP 5 or the
factors in STEP 11-C or both:

L. ADD Line J and Line K: $_____

The amount on Line L is the amount of child support to be paid by the
non-custodial parent to the custodial parent for all costs of the children, except
for child care expenses, health care expenses, and college, post-secondary,
private, special or enriched education.

STEP 9
SPECIAL NUMERICAL FACTORS

CHILD CARE EXPENSES

M. Cost of child care resulting from custodial
parent's:

____ seeking work
____ working
____ attending elementary education
____ attending secondary education
____ attending higher education
____ attending vocational training
      leading to employment: $_____

N. MULTIPLY Line M by Line I: $_____

This is the amount the non-custodial parent must contribute to the custodial
parent for child care.

HEALTH EXPENSES

O. Reasonable future health care expenses not
covered by insurance: $_____

P. MULTIPLY Line O by Line I: $_____

This is the amount the non-custodial parent must contribute to the custodial
parent for health care or pay directly to the health care provider.

Q. EDUCATIONAL EXPENSES

(if appropriate, see STEP 11(b)): $_____

STEP 10
LOW INCOME EXEMPTIONS

R. INSERT amount of noncustodial
parent's income from Line E or Line $_____
F:

S. ADD amounts on Line L, Line N, $_____
Line P and Line Q (This total is
"basic child support"):

T. SUBTRACT Line S from Line R: $_____

If Line T is more than the self-support reserve*, then the low income
exemptions do not apply and child support remains as determined in Steps 8
and 9. If so, go to Step 11.

If Line T is less than the poverty level**, then:

U. INSERT amount of non-custodial $_____
parent's income from Line E or
Line F:

V. Self-support reserve: $_____

W. SUBTRACT Line V from Line U: $_____

If Line W is more than $300 per year, then Line W is the amount of basic child
support. If Line W is less than $300 per year, then basic child support must be
a minimum of $300 per year.

If Line T is less than the self-support reserve* but more than the poverty
level**, then:

X. INSERT amount of noncustodial $_____
parent's income from Line E or Line
F:

Y. Self-support reserve: $_____

Z. SUBTRACT Line Y from Line X: $_____

If Line Z is more than $600 per year, then Line Z is the amount of basic child
support. If Line Z is less than $600 per year, then basic child support must be a
minimum of $600 per year.

*The self-support reserve. This figure changes on April 1 of each year. The
current self-support reserve is 135% of the office Federal poverty level for a
single person household as promulgated by the U.S. Department of Health and
Human Services.

**The poverty level. This figure changes on April 1 of each year. The current
Federal poverty level for a single person household in any year is as
promulgated by the U.S. Department of Health and Human Services.

STEP 11

NON-NUMERICAL FACTORS

(a) NON-RECURRING INCOME

A portion of non-recurring income, such as life insurance proceeds, gifts and inheritances or lottery winnings, may be allocated to child support. The law does not mention a specific percentage for such non-recurring income. Such support is not modified by the low income exemptions.

(b) EDUCATIONAL EXPENSES

New York's child support law does not contain a specific percentage method to determine how parents should share the cost of education of their children. Traditionally, the courts have considered both parents' complete financial circumstances in deciding who pays how much. The most important elements of financial circumstances are income, reasonable expenses, and financial resources such as savings and investments.

(c) ADDITIONAL FACTORS

The child support guidelines law lists 10 factors that should be considered in deciding on the amount of child support for:

____ combined incomes of more than $80,000 per year or

____ to vary the numerical result of these steps because the result is "unjust or inappropriate".

However, any court order deviating from the guidelines must set forth the amount of "basic child support" (Line S) resulting from the Guidelines and the reason for the deviation.

These factors are:

1. The financial resources of the parents and the child.

2. The physical and emotional health of the child and his/her special needs and aptitudes.

3. The standard of living the child would have enjoyed if the marriage or household was not dissolved.

4. The tax consequences to the parents.

5. The non-monetary contributions the parents will make toward the care and well-being of the child.

6. The educational needs of the parents.

7. The fact that the gross income of one parent is substantially less than the gross income of the other parent.

8. The needs of the other children of the non-custodial parent for whom the non-custodial parent is providing support, but only (a) if Line 23 is not deducted; (b) after considering the financial resources of any other person obligated to support the other children; and (c) if the resources available to support the other children are less then the resources available to support the children involved in this matter.

9. If a child is not on public assistance, the amount of extraordinary costs of visitation (such as out-of-state travel) or extended visits (other than the usual two to four week summer visits), but only if the custodial parent's expenses are substantially reduced by the visitation involved.

10. Any other factor the court decides is relevant.

NON-JUDICIAL DETERMINATION OF CHILD SUPPORT

Outside of court, parents are free to agree to any amount of support, so long as they sign a statement that they have been advised of the provisions of the child support guidelines law, the amount of "basic child support" (Line S) resulting from the Guidelines and the reason for any deviation. Further, the Court must approve any deviation, and the court cannot approve agreements of less than $300 per year. This minimum is not per child, meaning that the minimum for 3 children is $300 per year, not $900 per year. In addition, the courts retain discretion over child support.[1]

---

1   Source: New York State Unified Court System.

APPENDIX 22:
SAMPLE QUALIFIED MEDICAL CHILD
SUPPORT ORDER

PRESENT: Hon. _____
                    Justice/Referee

_____
                    Plaintiff,   Index No. _____

-against-   **QUALIFIED MEDICAL
                                                   CHILD SUPPORT ORDER**

                    Defendant.
_____

NOTICE: YOUR WILLFUL FAILURE TO OBEY THIS ORDER MAY, AFTER A COURT HEARING, RESULT IN YOUR COMMITMENT TO JAIL FOR A TERM NOT TO EXCEED SIX MONTHS, FOR CONTEMPT OF COURT.

Pursuant to [recite applicable section of law]. This Qualified Medical Child Support Order (QMCSO) orders and directs that the unemancipated dependents named herein:

Name:
Date of Birth:
Soc. Sec.#:
Mailing Address:

are entitled to be enrolled in and receive the benefits for which the legally responsible relative named herein is eligible, under the group health plan named herein in accordance with Section 609 of the Federal Employee Retirement Income Security Act.

The Participant (legally responsible relative) is:

Name:
Soc. Sec.#:
Mailing Address:

The Dependents' Custodial Parent or Legal Guardian who is to be provided with any identification cards and benefit claim forms on behalf of dependents:

Name:
Soc. Sec.#:
Mailing Address:

The group health plan subject to this order is:

Name:
Address:
Identification No.:

The administrator of said plan is:

Name:
Address:

The type of coverage provided is: [set forth coverage, e.g. medical, dental, etc.]

ORDERED that coverage shall include all plans covering the health, medical, dental, pharmaceutical and optical needs of the aforementioned Dependents named above for which the Participant is eligible.

ORDERED that said coverage shall be effective as of (give date) and shall continue as available until the respective emancipation of the aforementioned dependents.

ENTER:

JUSTICE/REFEREE

TO: [Health Insurer]

NOTICE: Pursuant to applicable law, if an employer, organization or group health plan fails to enroll eligible dependents or to deduct from the debtor's income the debtor's share of the premium, such employer, organization or group health plan administrator shall be jointly and severally liable for all medical expenses incurred on behalf of the debtor's dependents named in the execution while such dependents are not so enrolled to the extent of the insurance benefits that should have been provided under such execution.

The group health plan is not required to provide any type or form of benefit or option not otherwise provided under the group health plan except to the extent necessary to meet the requirements of a law relating to medical child support described in section one thousand three hundred and ninety six g-1 of title forty-two of the United States Code.[1]

---

1   Source: New York State Unified Court System.

APPENDIX 23:
SAMPLE INCOME DEDUCTION ORDER

SUPREME COURT OF THE STATE OF NEW YORK
COUNTY OF

_____ x

                         Plaintiff,   **Index No.**_____

   -against-

                                 INCOME DEDUCTION ORDER

                       Defendant.

_____ x

ORDERED that the payments required by the support order issued simultaneously herewith shall be withheld by the debtor's employer from the debtor's compensation, made payable to the creditor identified below and sent to:

Payee: _____
Address: _____

Debtor: Name:_____

             Address: _____

             Social Security No.:_____

Creditor: Name: _____
             Address: _____

             Social Security No.:_____

Debtor's Employer:_____

_____

Amount to be withheld: $_____ per _____

Date of Termination of Payments: _____

Dated: _____

SO ORDERED:

_____

Justice

_____

Source: New York State Unified Court System.

APPENDIX 24:
DIVORCE STATUTES—CUSTODY CRITERIA

JURISDICTION	FACTORS CONSIDERED
Alabama	Statutory guidelines; children's wishes; joint custody; domestic violence
Alaska	Statutory guidelines; children's wishes; joint custody; cooperative parent; domestic violence; health
Arizona	Statutory guidelines; children's wishes; joint custody; cooperative parent; domestic violence; health
Arkansas	Domestic violence
California	Statutory guidelines; children's wishes; cooperative parent; domestic violence; health
Colorado	Statutory guidelines; children's wishes; cooperative parent; joint custody; domestic violence; health
Connecticut	Children's wishes; joint custody
Delaware	Statutory guidelines; children's wishes; health
District of Columbia	Statutory guidelines; children's wishes; joint custody; cooperative parent; domestic violence; health
Florida	Statutory guidelines; children's wishes; joint custody; cooperative parent; domestic violence; health
Georgia	Statutory guidelines; children's wishes; joint custody; domestic violence
Hawaii	Statutory guidelines; children's wishes; joint custody; domestic violence
Idaho	Statutory guidelines; children's wishes; joint custody; domestic violence; health
Illinois	Statutory guidelines; children's wishes; joint custody; cooperative parent; domestic violence; health

JURISDICTION	FACTORS CONSIDERED
Indiana	Statutory guidelines; children's wishes; joint custody; cooperative parent; domestic violence; health
Iowa	Statutory guidelines; children's wishes; joint custody; cooperative parent; domestic violence; health
Kansas	Statutory guidelines; children's wishes; joint custody; cooperative parent; domestic violence; health
Kentucky	Statutory guidelines; children's wishes; joint custody; cooperative parent; domestic violence; health
Louisiana	Statutory guidelines; children's wishes; joint custody; domestic violence
Maine	Statutory guidelines; children's wishes; joint custody; domestic violence
Maryland	Children's wishes; joint custody; cooperative parent; domestic violence; health
Massachusetts	Joint custody; domestic violence
Michigan	Statutory guidelines; children's wishes; joint custody; cooperative parent; domestic violence; health
Minnesota	Statutory guidelines; children's wishes; joint custody; domestic violence; health
Mississippi	Statutory guidelines; joint custody; health
Missouri	Statutory guidelines; children's wishes; joint custody; cooperative parent; domestic violence; health
Montana	Statutory guidelines; children's wishes; joint custody; domestic violence
Nebraska	Statutory guidelines; children's wishes; joint custody; domestic violence; health
Nevada	Statutory guidelines; children's wishes; joint custody; cooperative parent; domestic violence
New Hampshire	Statutory guidelines; children's wishes; joint custody; domestic violence
New Jersey	Statutory guidelines; children's wishes; joint custody; cooperative parent; domestic violence; health
New Mexico	Statutory guidelines; children's wishes; joint custody; cooperative parent; domestic violence; health
New York	Children's wishes; domestic violence

JURISDICTION	FACTORS CONSIDERED
North Carolina	Children's wishes; joint custody; domestic violence; health
North Dakota	Statutory guidelines; children's wishes; joint custody; cooperative parent; domestic violence; health
Ohio	Statutory guidelines; children's wishes; joint custody; domestic violence; health
Oklahoma	Statutory guidelines; children's wishes; joint custody; cooperative parent; domestic violence
Oregon	Statutory guidelines; children's wishes; joint custody; cooperative parent; domestic violence
Pennsylvania	Statutory guidelines; children's wishes; joint custody; cooperative parent; domestic violence; health
Rhode Island	Children's wishes; joint custody; cooperative parent; domestic violence; health
South Carolina	Children's wishes; joint custody; cooperative parent; domestic violence; health
South Dakota	Children's wishes; joint custody; cooperative parent; domestic violence
Tennessee	Statutory guidelines; children's wishes; joint custody; cooperative parent; domestic violence
Texas	Statutory guidelines; children's wishes; joint custody; cooperative parent; domestic violence; health
Utah	Statutory guidelines; children's wishes; joint custody; cooperative parent
Vermont	Statutory guidelines joint custody; domestic violence
Virginia	Statutory guidelines; children's wishes; joint custody; cooperative parent; domestic violence; health
Washington	Statutory guidelines; children's wishes; domestic violence; health
West Virginia	Children's wishes; joint custody; domestic violence
Wisconsin	Statutory guidelines; children's wishes; joint custody; cooperative parent; domestic violence; health
Wyoming	Children's wishes; joint custody; domestic violence[1]

---

1   Source: American Bar Association, Family Law Section.

APPENDIX 25:
DIVORCE STATUTES—THIRD PARTY VISITATION AUTHORIZED BY STATUTE

JURISDICTION	PARTIES PERMITTED TO PETITION FOR THIRD PARTY VISITATION
Alabama	Grandparent in case of death of child; grandparent in case of divorce of child
Alaska	Stepparent; grandparent in case of death of child; grandparent in case of divorce of child; parent of child born out of wedlock; any interested party
Arizona	Stepparent; grandparent in case of death of child; grandparent in case of divorce of child; parent of child born out of wedlock; any interested party
Arkansas	Stepparent; grandparent in case of death of child; grandparent in case of divorce of child
California	Stepparent; grandparent in case of death of child; grandparent in case of divorce of child; any interested party
Colorado	Grandparent in case of death of child; grandparent in case of divorce of child; parent of child born out of wedlock
Connecticut	Stepparent; grandparent in case of death of child; grandparent in case of divorce of child; parent of child born out of wedlock; any interested party
Delaware	Stepparent; grandparent in case of divorce of child
District of Columbia	None listed
Florida	Grandparent in case of death of child; grandparent in case of divorce of child; parent of child born out of wedlock

JURISDICTION	PARTIES PERMITTED TO PETITION FOR THIRD PARTY VISITATION
Georgia	Grandparent in case of death of child; grandparent in case of divorce of child
Hawaii	Stepparent; grandparent in case of divorce of child
Idaho	Grandparent in case of divorce of child; parent of child born out of wedlock
Illinois	Stepparent; grandparent in case of death of child; grandparent in case of divorce of child; parent of child born out of wedlock
Indiana	Stepparent; grandparent in case of death of child; grandparent in case of divorce of child; parent of child born out of wedlock
Iowa	Grandparent in case of death of child; grandparent in case of divorce of child; parent of child born out of wedlock
Kansas	Stepparent; grandparent in case of death of child; grandparent in case of divorce of child; parent of child born out of wedlock
Kentucky	Grandparent in case of death of child; grandparent in case of divorce of child; parent of child born out of wedlock; any interested party
Louisiana	Stepparent under extraordinary circumstances; grandparent in case of death of child; grandparent in case of divorce of child
Maine	Stepparent; grandparent in case of death of child; grandparent in case of divorce of child; parent of child born out of wedlock
Maryland	Grandparent in case of death of child; grandparent in case of divorce of child
Massachusetts	Grandparent in case of death of child; grandparent in case of divorce of child; parent of child born out of wedlock
Michigan	Stepparent; grandparent in case of death of child; grandparent in case of divorce of child
Minnesota	Stepparent; grandparent in case of death of child; grandparent in case of divorce of child; parent of child born out of wedlock
Mississippi	Grandparent in case of death of child; grandparent in case of divorce of child

JURISDICTION	PARTIES PERMITTED TO PETITION FOR THIRD PARTY VISITATION
Missouri	Grandparent in case of death of child; grandparent in case of divorce of child; parent of child born out of wedlock
Montana	Grandparent in case of death of child; grandparent in case of divorce of child; parent of child born out of wedlock
Nebraska	Stepparent; grandparent in case of death of child; grandparent in case of divorce of child; parent of child born out of wedlock
Nevada	Grandparent in case of death of child; grandparent in case of divorce of child; parent of child born out of wedlock
New Hampshire	Stepparent; grandparent in case of death of child; grandparent in case of divorce of child; parent of child born out of wedlock
New Jersey	Stepparent; grandparent in case of death of child; grandparent in case of divorce of child; parent of child born out of wedlock
New Mexico	Stepparent; grandparent in case of death of child; grandparent in case of divorce of child; parent of child born out of wedlock; any interested party
New York	Stepparent; grandparent in case of death of child; grandparent in case of divorce of child; parent of child born out of wedlock
North Carolina	Grandparent in case of divorce of child
North Dakota	Stepparent; grandparent in case of death of child; grandparent in case of divorce of child; parent of child born out of wedlock
Ohio	Stepparent; grandparent in case of death of child; grandparent in case of divorce of child; parent of child born out of wedlock; interested third party provided they are related to minor child
Oklahoma	Grandparent in case of death of child; grandparent in case of divorce of child; parent of child born out of wedlock
Oregon	Stepparent; grandparent in case of death of child; grandparent in case of divorce of child; parent of child born out of wedlock; any interested party

JURISDICTION	PARTIES PERMITTED TO PETITION FOR THIRD PARTY VISITATION
Pennsylvania	Grandparent in case of death of child; grandparent in case of divorce of child
Rhode Island	Grandparent in case of death of child; grandparent in case of divorce of child
South Carolina	Grandparent in case of death of child; grandparent in case of divorce of child; parent of child born out of wedlock
South Dakota	Grandparent in case of death of child; grandparent in case of divorce of child; parent of child born out of wedlock
Tennessee	Stepparent; Grandparent in case of divorce of child
Texas	Stepparent; grandparent in case of death of child; grandparent in case of divorce of child; parent of child born out of wedlock; any interested party
Utah	Stepparent; grandparent in case of death of child; grandparent in case of divorce of child; parent of child born out of wedlock; any interested party
Vermont	Grandparent in case of death of child; grandparent in case of divorce of child
Virginia	Interested third party
Washington	Stepparent; grandparent in case of divorce of child
West Virginia	Grandparent in case of death of child; grandparent in case of divorce of child; parent of child born out of wedlock
Wisconsin	Grandparent in case of divorce of child
Wyoming	Stepparent; grandparent in case of death of child; grandparent in case of divorce of child; parent of child born out of wedlock; any interested party[1]

1   Source: American Bar Association, Family Law Section.

GLOSSARY

Abandonment—A ground for divorce. Abandonment occurs when the Defendant has willfully left the Plaintiff continuously, usually for a period of one year or more, without the plaintiff's consent.

Adultery—A ground for divorce. Adultery is any sexual act or deviate sexual act with a partner other than the spouse.

Affidavit of Service—An oath that litigation papers were properly served upon the opposing party.

Ancillary Relief—Additional or supplemental relief sought in a divorce action, such as custody, child support, etc.

Annulment—To make void by competent authority.

Arrears—Money which is overdue and unpaid.

Bigamy—The criminal offense of willfully and knowingly contracting a second marriage while the first marriage is still undissolved.

Calendar Number—This number is assigned by the court to an action upon the filing of the final papers for divorce with the court.

Child Custody—The care, control and maintenance of a child which may be awarded by a court to one of the parents of the child.

Child Support—The legal obligation of parents to contribute to the economic maintenance of their children.

Cohabit—To live together as husband and wife.

Cohabitation—The mutual assumption of those marital rights, duties and obligations which are usually manifested by married people.

Collusion—An agreement by two or more persons to obtain an object forbidden by law.

Commingle—To combine funds or property into a common fund.

Common-law Marriage—One not solemnized in the ordinary way but created by an agreement to marry followed by cohabitation.

Community Property—Property owned in common by husband and wife each having an undivided one-half interest by reason of their marital status.

Condonation—Conditional forgiveness, by means of continuance or resumption of marital cohabitation, by one of the married parties, of a known matrimonial offense committed by the other that would constitute a cause of divorce.

Constructive Abandonment—A ground for divorce. Constructive abandonment occurs when the defendant has refused to engage in sexual relations with the plaintiff, continuously, usually for a period of one year or more, without the plaintiff's consent.

Contested Divorce—A divorce action which is defended.

Contingent—Conditioned upon the occurrence of some future event.

Corroborate—To support a statement, argument, etc. with confirming facts or evidence.

Counterclaim—The defendant's response to the Verified Complaint, contained in the Verified Answer, which asserts the defendant's allegations of his or her own grounds for divorce against the plaintiff.

Cruel and Inhuman Treatment—A ground for divorce. Cruel and inhuman treatment consists of cruelty, whether physical, verbal, sexual or emotional, committed by the defendant, against the plaintiff, that endangers the plaintiff's well-being and makes living together either unsafe or improper.

Default Judgment—A divorce judgment may be obtained against the defendant when the defendant fails to respond to the summons and or complaint for divorce within the time allowed by law.

Defendant—The person whom the divorce is initiated against.

Divorce—The legal separation of a husband and wife, effected by the judgment or decree of a court.

Domestic Relations Law—Generally refers to the body of law that governing divorce and other matrimonial actions, also known as family or matrimonial law.

Ecclesiastical Law—The body of jurisprudence administered by the ecclesiastical courts of England derived from the canon and civil law.

Elective Share—Statutory provision that a surviving spouse may choose as between taking that which is provided in the spouse's will, or taking a statutorily prescribed share.

Emancipation—The surrender of care, custody and earnings of a child, as well as renunciation of parental duties.

Equitable Distribution—The power of the courts to equitably distribute all property legally and beneficially acquired during marriage by either spouse, whether legal title lies in their joint or individual names.

Fornication—Unlawful sexual intercourse between two unmarried persons.

Hearing—Proceeding with definite issues of fact or law to be tried in which witnesses and parties may be heard.

Illegitimacy—A child who is born at a time when his parents are not married to each other.

Incest—The crime of sexual intercourse or cohabitation between a man and woman who are related to each other within the degrees wherein marriage is prohibited by law.

Intestate—A person is said to die intestate when he or she dies without making a will.

Judgment of Divorce—A document signed by the court granting the divorce.

Justification—A just, lawful excuse or reason for an act or failing to act.

Maintenance—A term for spousal support; formerly referred to as alimony.

Marital Assets—Any property, regardless of which person is named as owner, that is acquired by the Plaintiff or Defendant from the date of marriage to the commencement of the divorce action., e.g., a house, car, IRA, joint bank account, pension or annuity.

Meretricious—An unlawful sexual connection.

Order of Protection—An order issued by a court that directs one individual to stop certain conduct, such as harassment, against another individual and that may order the individual to be excluded from the residence and to stay away from the other individual, his or her home, school, place of employment and his or her children.

Palimony—An award of support which arises out of the dissolution of a nonmarital relationship.

Paternity—The relationship of fatherhood.

Perjury—A crime where a person under oath swears falsely in a matter material to the issue or point in question.

Plaintiff—The person who starts the divorce action.

Poor Person Application—An application made to the court, by either the plaintiff or defendant, stating that because of insufficient income he or she is unable to pay the court fees normally required for divorce actions. If the application is granted by the court, the usual court costs for the divorce action are waived.

Prenuptial Agreement—An agreement entered into by prospective spouses prior to and in contemplation of marriage.

Procreation—The generation of children.

Provocation—The act of inciting another to do a particular deed.

Real Property—Land, and generally whatever is erected or growing upon or affixed to the land.

Recrimination—A counter-charge of adultery or cruelty made by the accused spouse in a suit for divorce against the accusing spouse.

Removal of Barriers to Remarriage—Refers to the removal of religious barriers to remarriage when the marriage was solemnized in a religious ceremony by a clergyman or minister of any religion.

Separate Property—Property owned by a married person in his or her own right during marriage.

Separation Agreement—Written arrangements concerning custody, child support, spousal support, and property division usually made by a married couple who decide to live separate and apart in contemplation of divorce.

Spousal Maintenance—Money paid by one spouse to another for living expenses.

Uncontested Divorce—A divorce action in which the defendant does not respond to the summons or otherwise agrees not to oppose the divorce.

Verified Answer—The defendant's response to the Verified Complaint. The principal difference between a Verified Answer and a counterclaim in a divorce action is that a Verified Answer responds only to the allegations of the Verified Complaint, whereby a counterclaim is added to the Verified Answer to additionally allege that the defendant seeks a divorce from the plaintiff.

Verified Complaint—The document containing the plaintiff's allegations of his or her grounds for divorce.

Visitation—The right of one parent to visit children of the marriage under order of the court.

Void—Having no legal force or binding effect.

Voidable—That which may be declared void but is not absolutely void or void in itself.

BIBLIOGRAPHY

American Bar Association Commission: Family Law Section (Date Visited: September 2001) <http://www.abanet.org/>.

American Civil Liberties Union (Date Visited: September 2001) <http://www.aclu.org/>.

Black's Law Dictionary, Fifth Edition. St. Paul, MN: West Publishing Company, 1979.

Editors of the Family Law Reporter, Desk Guide to the Uniform Marriage and Divorce Act. Washington, D.C.: The Bureau of National Affairs, Inc., 1974, rev. 1982.

Green, Samuel and Long, John V., Marriage and Family Law Agreements. Colorado Springs, CO: Shepards/McGraw Hill, 1984, rev. 1992.

Handbook on Child Support Enforcement. U.S. Department of Health and Human Services, Office of Child Support Enforcement, 1989.

Samuelson, Elliot D., The Divorce Law Handbook. New York, NY: Insight Books/Human Services Press, Inc., 1988.

Legal Information Institute (Date Visited: September 2001) <http://www.law.cornell.edu/>.